Praise for Paul Frenkel's

LIFE RECLAIMED

LIFE RECLAIMED is an inspiring, uplifting, and important human story. It is a completely unpretentious, straightforward, and engaging picture of life, hope, and persistence in the face of depravity and the basest of inhumanities. Paul Frenkel's integrity and honesty, expressed with clarity and simplicity, captivate and elevate the reader.

LIFE RECLAIMED is not a polemic; it is not bitter or angry. Without a trace of self consciousness, Paul Frenkel draws the reader into a wonderful relationship with an innocent young boy in rural Transylvania. Engaged with Paul as an empathetic friend, we are gripped as we walk with him through the innocence, the unimaginable horrors, and then the path traveled toward the reclamation of life underscores the power and beauty of life itself.

It has been my privilege and blessing to have had Paul Frenkel and his family in my life these past 33 years. I am proud to be among those who present this blessed human being to you.

Rabbi Norman Koch
Temple Sholom, New Milford, CT

In Paul Frenkel's **LIFE RECLAIMED** the author offers a compelling personal testimony of pre-Holocaust rural Transylvania, the nightmare of the Holocaust's victims, and their struggle to find meaningful lives after World War Two. Surprisingly, the pre-war portrait depicts a community of mutual respect and celebration of difference, in which Hungarians, Rumanians, Germans, Jews, and Gypsies lived side by side. Such civil society proved fragile. Only the exceptionally strong, young, and just plain lucky among Holocaust victims survived. Few of the survivors re-established a quality of life which equaled their pre-war origins. Even the few who attained post-war success evidence deep scars in their faith in humanity, as Frenkel testifies. He challenges the world to prove that the Holocaust was an aberration, 'never again' to be repeated. Unfortunately, Cambodia, Sri Lanka, Bosnia, Rwanda, and Darfur justify Frenkel's pessimism about human nature.

Rabbi Mark L. Winer, Ph.D., D.D.
President, FAITH: the Foundation to Advance Interfaith
Trust and Harmony; Chairman, International Interfaith Task
Force of the World Union for Progressive Judaism; Past
President, National Council of Synagogues of America

LIFE RECLAIMED presents a clear and human picture of the shocking impact of the holocaust on young Paul Frenkel whose happy, normal life in a small Transylvanian town became a nightmare in an instant. Paul allows us to experience the Hungarian holocaust through his youthful eyes which immeasurably contributes to our understanding of the emotional impact of the holocaust on its victims. It is also a story of a teen ager's psychological and physical survival in a world gone mad. I found the book totally absorbing and insightful and I highly recommend it.

Mayor Earl Leiken
City of Shaker Heights, Ohio
Past President, Jewish Community Center of Greater Cleveland

LIFE RECLAIMED
Rural Transylvania, Nazi Camps, and the American Dream

Paul N. Frenkel

iUniverse, Inc.
Bloomington

LIFE RECLAIMED
RURAL TRANSYLVANIA, NAZI CAMPS, AND THE AMERICAN DREAM

iUniverse books may be ordered through booksellers or by contacting:

iUniverse
1663 Liberty Drive
Bloomington, IN 47403
www.iuniverse.com
1-800-Authors (1-800-288-4677)

Front Cover Photo:
Photograph of Paul Frenkel in July or August 1945, at about age sixteen, sitting on a rock in the Black Sea near Odessa where Uncle Feri took him for a brief vacation in July or August 1945, a few months after his escape from the Berga death march.

Back Cover Photo:
A 1943 photograph of the Frenkel family taken in Szamosujvar (Gherla), Hungary, showing brother Gabriel, mother Ida, father Morice, and Paul.

ISBN: 978-1-4759-8027-1 (sc)
ISBN: 978-1-4759-8028-8 (hc)
ISBN: 978-1-4759-8029-5 (e)

Library of Congress Control Number: 2013904244

Printed in the United States of America

iUniverse rev. date: 3/15/2013

For the family I have lost, and the family I have found: my wife, Rita; my daughter, Victoria, her husband, Tom, and my grandsons Theo and Simon; and my son, Nicholas, his wife, Nanci, and my grandsons Oliver and Logan.

TABLE OF CONTENTS

MAPS, FRENKEL FAMILY TREE, AND PHOTO ALBUM

ACKNOWLEDGMENTS

I am greatly indebted to Sean Seagrave for drawing the maps and mounting the photographs. I also want to thank the following people for reading the manuscript and providing their many helpful suggestions: Rita Frenkel, Susan Plaeger, Bernard Casey, Jocelyn Seagrave, Mimi O'Connor (who also prepared the Frenkel family tree), Earl and Ellen Leiken, Norton and Pat Baron, Charles Yonkers, William Corcoran, Peter Healey, George and Deborah Chaconas, Professor Francis Ambrosio, Ayelet Waldman, Christina Larocco, Ron Chambers, Peter Gray, Marge Neuwirth, and Melinda Heslop. I also want to acknowledge the labors of Christine Schmidt, who singlehandedly has researched and provided the physical data about the Berga camp and death march, and who presently is researching approximately 120 other death marches.

Finally, and most of all, I want to thank my longtime friend and lawyer Chuck O'Connor (Charles A. O'Connor III) for researching the history, helping to organize the memoir, and turning my written and oral narrative into clear prose.

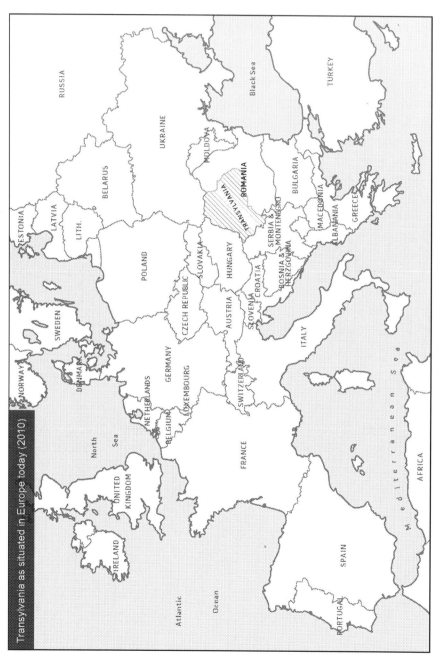

Map 1: Transylvania as situated in Europe today (2010).

PROLOGUE
Remembrance of Things Past

In April 1944, during the last year of World War II and two months before the D-day landings at Normandy, I was a fourteen-year-old living happily with my family in the rural Transylvanian town of Hadad, Hungary. Suddenly, and without explanation or justification, I was rounded up with my family and other Hungarian Jews, confined in a factory yard, and then herded into cattle cars and shipped off to Auschwitz. Just recalling these fateful events evokes disturbing images—the omnipresent death and brutality at the Auschwitz, Buchenwald, Zeitz, and Berga concentration camps and, finally, the death march at the war's end, when the Nazis forced those prisoners still alive out of the camps and onto aimless journeys intended to weaken them from exertion and starvation before they were executed as they fell by the wayside.

Once again, I see myself wearing a thin, striped uniform and marching among hundreds of weak and malnourished Berga prisoners herded toward some unknown destination. We trudged at gunpoint in bitterly cold weather through the mountainous terrain of Sudetenland, heading into Czechoslovakia and away from the sound of distant artillery fire from the advancing Russian armies. As our Nazi guards shot the slow-moving and dying at the rear of the march, I survived to eventually escape only because I remained at the head of the line.

It wasn't until 1982, when I was fifty-three, that I ever spoke to anyone, even my immediate family and closest friends, about my experience of Hitler's "final solution" for the Jews. I was just a young teenager when the Nazis murdered my parents, grandparents, aunt, uncle, and many other relatives. They imprisoned me as a slave laborer in four different concentration camps and then forced me on a death march into Czechoslovakia. This was a dark and disturbing past, and I had tried to bury it. What finally pushed me to break my silence was a letter to the editor by a Holocaust denier—published in our local Connecticut newspaper, the *New Milford Times*—claiming that the Holocaust never happened. I could not let this falsehood go unchallenged, so I wrote a reply that the newspaper published. Thus, thirty-seven years after the Holocaust, I had finally identified myself as a survivor.

About three years later, my twelve-year-old son, Nicholas, came looking for me one day after school. His class was studying the Holocaust by reading Elie Wiesel's *Night,* and his teacher wanted me to talk to the class about my World War II experience. Like Wiesel, I was a Transylvanian Jew who had endured and outlasted the Nazi concentration camps. Now that my long-held secret was out, I had to confront the prospect of speaking publicly about my painful past. At the very least, if I chose to say nothing more, I had to tell Nicholas my reasons for declining his teacher's invitation. Why had I hidden this part of my life for so long? Was it still too painful to discuss, and if so, why—after so many years, a successful business career, a wonderful marriage, and two lovely children?

These troubling questions brought me back to September 5, 1949, when I arrived at the Port of New York with ten dollars in my pocket, a small briefcase holding all my worldly possessions, and the names of three uncles and a cousin whom I had never met. With my immediate family almost entirely gone, my Jewish heritage a source of inexplicable enmity, and only a few words of spoken English, I worried about my prospects in America. Perhaps, at least until I found my place here, I should change my last name, as other relatives had done, in order to mask who I was. Better to hide my identity, keep silent about my past, and thereby avoid the pain and ostracism, or so I thought at the time.

While pondering Nicholas's request, I had to acknowledge that during my many years of business dealings with the United States military, I had never felt any discrimination because of my religion. Perhaps I did not appear Jewish, or my many successful government contracts had removed suspicion, or Americans just did not care about my religion as Europeans had. No one but another survivor, I assumed, could empathize with my experience. On further reflection, however, I concluded that it was the pain of remembering things past that had kept me silent all these years. Surely it was my conduct and character, not my religion, that mattered to my fellow Americans. Maybe the frenetic pace of managing my company's worldwide business was just a subconscious Band-Aid for this latent pain. Ultimately, I concluded that the time had come to confront the past and face the consequences. Furthermore, I felt an obligation to educate an uninformed younger generation about the wrongs perpetrated by a malevolent segment of an older generation.

So in 1985, I proceeded to address my son's seventh-grade class at Shepaug Valley High School in Washington, Connecticut. I did the same for my daughter Victoria's ninth-grade class at the Forman School in Litchfield, Connecticut. And I also gave a six-hour videotaped interview on invitation from Yale, where I heard Elie Wiesel speak. Thereafter, for several years, I spoke to groups of other Litchfield-area students who were trying to understand the Holocaust. My views even became part of a written exchange on the subject published by Skidmore College. Yet the experience eventually proved disheartening. I found that high-school students were interested in those remote events more for their superficial adventure than their intrinsic evil and attendant human suffering. I became offended by, and refused to endure, trivial questions like "Did you ever meet Hitler?" and "Was the food good in the death camps?" Instead of catharsis, I had found frustration—now centered on the indifference of students apparently too young to understand the seriousness of the issue or to recognize the Holocaust as a monstrous crime.

In 1998, plaintiff lawyers began filing class-action suits before Judge Edward R. Korman in the federal district court in Brooklyn, New York, on behalf of survivors who sought compensation for their slave labor or restitution for their stolen wealth. I poured my new frustration and anger into this litigation. I testified about my own experience, and I marched to publicize the unremedied offenses of German businesses that had enslaved Jewish laborers and of Swiss banks that had profited from stolen Jewish assets. I traveled to Washington, DC, for the settlement negotiations with the foreign defendants by Stuart Eizenstat at the US State Department, but I was barred from participating. A State Department representative explained that having a victim present would complicate negotiations with the Germans, but I felt that the United States really wanted to preserve Germany's goodwill in support of its ongoing dealings with the Russians. I was left standing outside the room, not even allowed to observe the negotiations, and I returned home further frustrated.

Under a settlement with German companies, Jewish-American GIs interred with us in Berga Concentration Camp were awarded $75,000 to $100,000 each. Yet the special master, Judge Sidney Gribetz, told me at a meeting of noncombatant survivors in New York City that Jewish slave laborers, like my brother Gabriel and me, would get "peanuts." This insulting prospective award resulted from the relatively miniscule allocation of the fund to US survivors due to Judge Korman's withholding of a portion and distributing other portions of the award in such a seemingly arbitrary fashion. Rather than suffer the affront, I opted out of the settlement and withdrew from the litigation.

Once again, I became disillusioned. The only real beneficiaries of this draining litigation seemed to be the lawyers, volunteer organizations, and civil libertarians—not the victims. My frustration and anger mounted. The establishment was not righting these grave wrongs or providing meaningful relief for numerous survivors, including the destitute. So I went public with my experiences, looking for other forms of relief. I undertook to sensitize the hardened public about the horrors inflicted by the Nazis on camp internees and to refocus the "volunteer" plaintiff lawyers on seeking a genuine remedy for the victims.

In April 1997, I gave an interview from my home to a film crew from Steven Spielberg's Shoah Foundation. In addition, I wrote a letter to the Swedish company SKF seeking restitution for victims like myself who worked in an SKF warehouse. During World War II, SKF supplied 70 percent of all Germany's steel imports, including ball bearings. For several months in the fall of 1944, I was a slave laborer at Zeitz Concentration Camp, carrying and stacking heavy boxes of SKF ball bearings. In its letter of reply, SKF denied it had such a warehouse.

I even wrote letters to the first President Bush and to the State Department, urging them to pursue just settlements with foreign governments for involuntary servitude and property theft. I thought that some meaningful level of financial compensation would constitute at least an acknowledgment of wrongdoing. Nothing came of all these efforts. On later reflection, moreover, no identifiable remedy seemed commensurate with the offenses, and these futile efforts only deepened my disillusionment. There seemed to be no prospect of ever satisfactorily redressing the unspeakable crimes of the Third Reich that I had witnessed and suffered.

A turning point came during a leisurely conversation one sunny fall afternoon in 2002 in the backyard of my friend Chuck O'Connor, a lawyer in Washington, DC. Chuck's firm had long represented me and my business in dealings with the US military. He urged that I not give up but, instead, tell my story for the sake of family, posterity, and my own sanity. Chuck also offered to help me write, edit, and publish it. Thus, at age seventy-three, I forfeited my last excuse, overcame my reluctance, and began the slow, agonizing, and halting process of writing this memoir. The words did not come easily, because reliving these horrors so long submerged in consciousness was torturous. Chuck often had to drag the details out of me in long interview sessions. Having finally reached publication, the memoir, I hope, will enlist public support for the remaining Nazi victims who are still denied adequate compensation for their slave labor and stolen property, despite the German and Swiss settlements. Perhaps publication also will exorcise my own personal demons. But most importantly, I hope it effectively highlights a dark corner of recent history so that such a thing may never recur.

PART I: THE SETTING

And as I was green and carefree, famous among the barns
About the happy yard and singing as the farm was home,
In the sun that is young once only,
Time let me play and be
Golden in the mercy of his means …

Dylan Thomas, "Fern Hill"

1.
Pastoral Hadad

Looking back today, I cannot imagine a happier childhood than growing up in our small agricultural community in remote northern Transylvania. I lived there until age fourteen with my parents Morice and Ida Frenkel and my brother, Gabriel. Hadad was a farming town of approximately two thousand people located in the foothills of the Carpathian Mountains. To most Americans, Transylvania conjures up gothic Hollywood tales of Count Dracula and vampires. To me, it provided the familiar comforts and endless fascination of rural farm life—horse-drawn carts, ancient dirt roads, Protestant church choirs, colorful Gypsy fiddlers, Tuesday produce markets, open-sleigh rides, and the weekly town crier.

Transylvania is the Latin word for the region, meaning "land beyond the forest"—those great forests that cover the Carpathian Mountains. The Carpathians provide Transylvania's huge natural border on the north, east, and south, leaving it open on the west to the Great Hungarian Plain. Transylvania consists of rolling hills, river valleys, and fertile plains, interrupted only by the Bihar Mountains near its center, just west of its historic capital city, Kolozsvar (now called Cluj-Napoca). Hadad lies near the very northern tip of Transylvania on a virtual straight line between the border city of Szatmar (Satu Mare), about twenty-five miles to the north, and the capital city of Kolozsvar, about fifty miles to the south (see Map 2).

Called "Hodod" by the Romanians and "Kriegsdorf" by the Germans, Hadad, as the Hungarians called it, was settled in the latter half of the eighteenth century by a Hungarian (or Magyar) nobleman named Wesselenyi, along with Lutherans from southern Germany. Wesselenyi's descendant, Count Banfi, owned a magnificent castle situated on the western side of town at the highest point in Hadad, about half a mile above the valley below. Count Banfi also owned most of the land in our part of Transylvania, and everything on it. This included all the animals (pigs, cattle, sheep, chickens, and horses), all the crops (fields of grains, fruit orchards, and a vineyard), all the forests, and the flour mill. What did not belong to Count Banfi belonged to Count Degenfeld, an absentee German landlord. Degenfeld Castle, located at the southern end of town, lay relatively dormant and largely unoccupied, except for the estate manager plus the caretaker and his family.

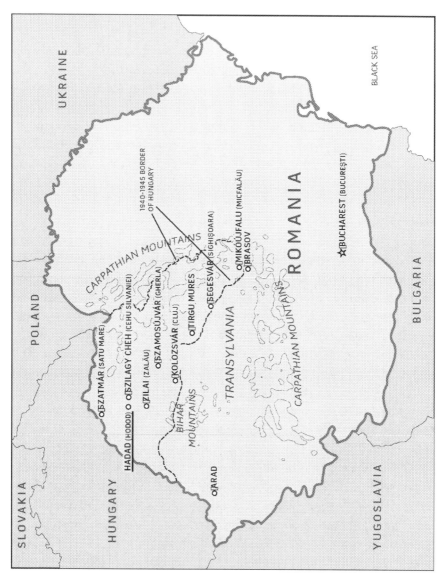

Map 2: This map shows modern-day Romania—including Transylvania, which falls within the arc of the Carpathian Mountains on the north, east, and south and the Hungarian border on the west. The dotted outline demarks the northern portion of Transylvania, which the Third Reich conveyed to Hungary in the Second Vienna Award of August 30, 1940, where it remained until the end of World War II. The map identifies those cities within northern Transylvania that factor in my early life, using their Hungarian names followed by their current Romanian names in parentheses.

Hadad covered a mile-wide stretch atop a gentle east-west hill and extended south about two miles down into a small valley with sprawling fields. The weather was ever-changing, and everyone's daily preoccupation. In summer, the weather was generally pleasant, especially for a youngster like me. But in winter, a brisk Siberian wind blew across the Carpathians into Transylvania, bringing biting cold winds and heavy snowfalls that drove everyone indoors. We huddled before the fireplace, well supplied with stacked wood, which was freely available and easy pickings in the nearby forests—at least before the first blizzard arrived. Rarely did people venture out in deep snow, except to feed the barn animals or to purchase flour and cooking oil from the mill.

The dramatic seasonal changes in Transylvanian weather captivated me. In fall, the leaves formed such a thick ground cushion that I could painlessly slide or roll down the long, steep embankments on the Banfi estate. When the weather turned cold, my leather shoes froze, clicked, and squeaked—clear signals to get indoors before my feet became frostbitten. The winter snowfall was often so heavy that the roads were impassable even for horse-drawn sleighs. When severe weather forced me inside, I played chess, arranged my stamp collection, and peered through Father's medical books to read about various diseases.

Throughout most of the winter, Hadad was perfect for sledding. My friends and I whisked down the main road through the town center and then turned down one of the two side streets, speeding toward the valley below. We were unconcerned about traffic, since there were no automobiles and few sleighs. Trees posed the only real danger. Careening through orchard trees, some of my friends lost teeth on impact with the ubiquitous tree trunks. My sledding injury occurred near the entrance to my elementary school. To make it all the way to the school entrance, I had to lie flat on the sled in order to pass under a railing in front of the school. One time I forgot to duck and hit the railing so hard I was knocked unconscious. To this day, I still bear a slight dent on the top of my head.

From spring through fall, we had almost daily rain showers, which turned the town's unpaved streets to mud. Walking in the slippery mud was treacherous, since the roads were uneven, strewn with rocks, and lined on either side by shallow ditches. If the weather suddenly turned cold, animal footprints froze in the mud, which made the roads more uneven and dangerous. Most people went around town on foot, so shoes became mud-caked from the moment they hit the ground. Removing that mud before walking into your house was a necessary ritual. My practice was to scrape my shoes using a small pocketknife, and then to clean the knife with wood shavings.

Hadad's main road (then as now) enters town from the northwest near Banfi Castle at the top of the hill. It descends south to Degenfeld Castle, turns east through the town center, and continues east out of town about seven miles to Szilagy Cseh (Cehu Silvaniei), which has the nearest train station. As you head east along the main road from Banfi Castle toward the town center, you pass the synagogue, the pharmacy, the market square, Degenfeld Castle, four general stores, one of Hadad's two taverns, the blacksmith shop, the town hall, the post office, two schools, and the Protestant Reformed (Calvinist) Church (see Map 3). Two smaller roads head south off the main road and down into the valley below the town. At the west end of the main road (back toward Banfi Castle) are the flour mill and the monument to unknown soldiers who died in World War I. Most of these places factor prominently in my story.

The Hadad I remember seemed to exist in a time warp, cut off from the rest of the world and unchanged for hundreds of years. There was no electricity, no indoor plumbing or running water, no telephone, and no newspaper. I cannot recall ever seeing a new house being built or hearing of anyone moving into or out of town. People went everywhere on foot, crossing paths daily with other townsfolk—in the fields, orchards, and streets; inside the stores, schools, barns, and churches; at the two farmers' markets and the post office; and less often at funerals. As they passed by, people greeted one another with "Buna ziua" or "Jo napot" ("Good day" in Romanian and Hungarian, respectively). Gossip exchanged during chance meetings was—other than the town crier—the major source of information.

Even in the best of weather, Hadad's roads had little traffic. People walked or drove horse- or cattle-drawn carts to the mill, the market, or the fields. On a rare day, you might see a stray dog searching for food. Casual strollers were the exception; everyone walked with a purpose, heading

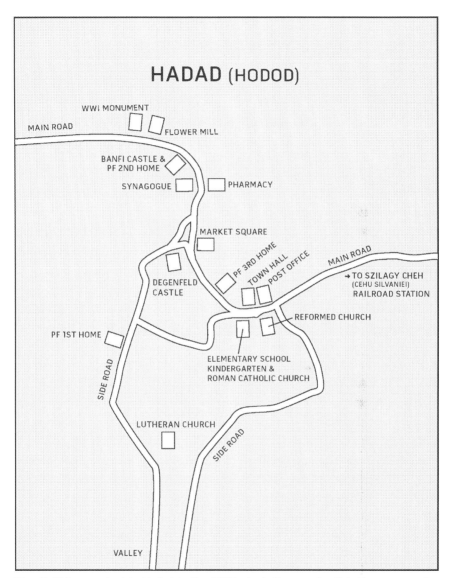

HADAD (HODOD)

WWI MONUMENT

MAIN ROAD

FLOWER MILL

BANFI CASTLE & PF 2ND HOME

SYNAGOGUE

PHARMACY

MARKET SQUARE

PF 3RD HOME

TOWN HALL

POST OFFICE

MAIN ROAD

DEGENFELD CASTLE

→ TO SZILAGY CHEH (CEHU SILVANIEI) RAILROAD STATION

REFORMED CHURCH

PF 1ST HOME

SIDE ROAD

ELEMENTARY SCHOOL KINDERGARTEN & ROMAN CATHOLIC CHURCH

LUTHERAN CHURCH

SIDE ROAD

VALLEY

Map 3: This map depicts Hadad in the 1940s, including our family's three successive homes, Banfi and Degenfeld castles, the Reformed and Lutheran churches, and the Jewish synagogue.

somewhere. Sundays and holidays, however, were special. On these days, young girls went arm-in-arm dressed in colorful Hungarian costumes, and peasants emerged in native attire all headed to the town square. There they danced to a Gypsy band composed of violins, flutes, clarinets, and solo accordion. The merriment was uplifting.

The only traffic congestion occurred at sunset during spring and summer when herds of cattle, sheep, and pigs returned home from pasture right through the center of the town. At the edge of town, using a special signal understood only by his dogs, the shepherd ordered his dogs away from the front of the pack. This triggered a stampede down the main street through the town center, forcing pedestrians to leap aside to safety. Each animal let out a sound as it scrambled for an unobstructed path. The pigs ran frantically ahead of the outnumbered, plodding cattle, each bent on securing its place at the awaiting trough of food. Caught in this organized chaos, pedestrians hugged the roadside until the last animal had passed.

In the 1940s, Hadad's ethnic and religious makeup was typical of small towns in northern Transylvania. It was predominantly Hungarian, with many Romanians, some Germans or Swabians (those Germans who populated the area during the eighteenth century), and still fewer Jews and Gypsies. Hadad had a variety of religions to match: Calvinist, Unitarian, Roman Catholic, Lutheran, and Jewish. Of Hadad's two thousand or so residents, fewer than a hundred were Jews. On Friday evenings, Saturday mornings, and holy days, the rabbi—wearing his usual long black coat and large fur hat and accompanied by his family—led a solemn procession from his home down the length of the main street to the synagogue, where he held services. Heading west through town, the procession passed directly in front of our home.

The local population consisted mostly of peasants who lived in small houses throughout town. Many peasants owned tiny plots of land, and a few had some cows and pigs, several chickens, possibly some geese, and in rare cases a horse. Almost everyone worked for the Banfi estate and depended on the land for his livelihood. Farm life was strenuous. Every job was manual, since farmers had no heavy equipment and used horses and cattle for plowing and hauling. I remember one man who developed a bad back and became a cripple from repeatedly loading and unloading heavy bags of grain. Those who did not work the land were tradesmen whose businesses depended on the peasants. Many of Hadad's tradesmen were Jewish.

Townspeople spent most of their time working in the fields or in their shops. Otherwise they remained at home. There was not much else to do. Department-store shopping and public entertainment, as we know them today, were nonexistent. And there were few social functions besides church on Sundays and holy days and synagogue on Friday evenings and Saturdays. Hadad had no theater, bookstore, or library—we borrowed our books from neighbors or friends. Even the schools and churches had very few textbooks and religious books. We had to read books hurriedly on the premises if we were going to read them at all. Some people frequented one of the two taverns in town, which served wine from wooden barrels and offered Gypsy music. The patrons sipped wine to the sound of violins, basses, cymbals, and the dulcimer (*cimbalom* in Hungarian). An open-air bowling alley located behind the main tavern featured competitive bowling on market days in summer. Despite its limited amenities, however, Hadad was seldom boring to me—never in good weather.

Today, Transylvania is part of Romania and has been throughout most of the twentieth century (see Map 1). Since the Middle Ages, however, Transylvania has generally been part of Hungary, and its long checkered history deserves a brief retelling because it affected life even in remote Hadad. Transylvania's history really begins in the year 987, when the Hungarian army under its commander Kolozs conquered the area and established Kolozsvar (the "Fort of Kolozs") as its capital. From the tenth to the sixteenth centuries, Transylvania was part of the Hungarian Kingdom, serving as its eastern frontier against the Ottoman Turks. In 1526, the Ottomans defeated the Hungarians and took control of Transylvania for the next 150 years. In the 1690s, the Ottomans ceded Transylvania to the Austro-Hungarian Empire, which oversaw Transylvania for the next 200 years. In 1867, Transylvania became reunited with Hungary, and they both remained part of the Austro-Hungarian Empire until the end of World War I. Then Transylvanian history becomes even more confusing.

Hungary and Austria picked the wrong side in World War I, whereas

Romania switched sides to the Allies in 1916, in exchange for postwar rights to Transylvania. The victorious Allies honored this agreement in the 1920 Treaty of Trianon, awarding Transylvania to Romania. Part of the justification for this award was the 1910 census, which indicated that Romanians constituted the majority of the Transylvanian population. Northern Transylvania, however, including Kolozsvar and the area above it (where Hadad is located), was primarily Hungarian. After Trianon, the Romanian government introduced discriminatory policies against Hungarians, banning the use of Hungarian place and street names and requiring that schools teach only in Romanian. Consequently, in 1920, Kolozsvar was renamed Cluj, and Hadad became Hodod. This anti-Hungarian discrimination lasted for two decades until the beginning of World War II and caused a latent animosity toward Romanians among the majority Hungarian population in Hadad.

In 1940, in appreciation for Hungary's military support, the Third Reich awarded northern Transylvania to Hungary, leaving southern Transylvania (below Cluj) with Romania (see Map 2). Consequently, in 1940, Cluj reverted to Kolozsvar and Hodod to Hadad, their original Hungarian names, and the official language in northern Transylvania changed back to Hungarian. Since most Hadad residents were Hungarian and virtually everyone spoke Hungarian, the language change had little practical impact on most people, including my family. My parents considered themselves of Hungarian origin; it was their native tongue and culture.

Transylvania remained divided between north and south from 1940 until late 1944, when the Russian army entered northern Transylvania. The Russians arrived several months after the Nazis had removed all of the Jewish people from the north, including my family. Toward the end of World War II, Romania again switched sides to the Allies and attacked Hungary. In reward for Romania's second wartime about-face, Russia returned northern Transylvania to Romania in 1945. The postwar Paris Peace Treaty of 1947 sanctioned this return, and ever since, Transylvania has remained part of Romania.

The 1920 and 1940 transitions to and from Romanian sovereignty, respectively, proved difficult for the citizens of Hadad. With each regime change, the mayor's nationality also changed, first to Romanian and then back to Hungarian, and the residents of that governing nationality reaped the benefits in political patronage. The 1940 power shift to the Hungarians spawned economic and political vendettas and score-settling among neighbors for actions taken during the prior two decades under Romanian rule. The historic animosity between the Hungarians and Romanians divided practically everyone in town. Though barely eleven years old in August 1940, I could feel the tension in Hadad when northern Transylvania transitioned back to Hungarian rule, even though I did not fully understand the politics.

The minority Germans, Jews, and Gypsies remained mostly spectators to this ethnic strife, but they could not wholly escape the fallout since they lived in its midst. The Germans, who constituted about 30 percent of the population, tended to live in the lower southern part of Hadad near the Lutheran Church. The Jews concentrated in the upper eastern part along the main street not far from the synagogue. The Gypsies lived in tents on the southern edge of town. The Hungarians and Romanians felt superior to both the Jews and Gypsies because the latter two had neither a separate country or homeland nor any obvious political or institutional defenders. The Jews posed no threat to participants in the running ethnic feud, however, since they were mostly tradesmen—shoemakers, tailors, tavern keepers, shopkeepers, and teachers—with limited incomes and no political aspirations.

Growing up in Hadad, I saw no great differences or distinctions among the Hungarians, Romanians, Germans, Jews, and Gypsies, and my religion never seemed to affect my relationships with any of them. Yet even as a child, I recognized the enormous class distinction between the vast majority of townspeople and the two local counts. With their impressive castles and vast inherited wealth, the counts enjoyed a unique social status. They lived in royal isolation, never venturing into town, and they traveled to and from Hadad by private carriage, which added to their mystique. No one in town ever expected to attain their status or wealth. At the opposite end of the social hierarchy were the peasants. Everyone else—professionals, clerics, and tradesmen—fell somewhere in between ... everyone, that is, except the Gypsies. They were generally considered outsiders.

Despite the ethnic and religious diversity of its population, Hadad itself had a remarkably similar look throughout, especially in its housing. Each house had at most two rooms: a kitchen and an adjoining sleeping-living room. The inside floors were mud and not level, undulating throughout the house with slight dips and rises. Inside the kitchen was a large mud-brick stove with an iron top, fed constantly with wood. The stove functioned not only for cooking but also for heating the entire house. Some houses also had a tall terra-cotta stove used solely for heating. On the top of the kitchen stove lay the wet clothes spread out to dry and the house cat fast asleep. Wood gathered from the forest served as the sole fuel for heating and cooking. Every season, my family bought logs from a farmer and hired an itinerant woodcutter to chop them into smaller pieces and stack them near the house. During winter, we carried armfuls inside daily to burn in the oven.

The numerous houses lining Hadad's main street and two principal secondary roads were all made of brick. Gypsies (*Cigany* in Hungarian) performed the construction work needed to maintain these houses. They made the bricks manually by mixing mud with cow dung and straw before scooping the mixture into wooden forms. Once the mud bricks became firm, they were removed from the forms to finish drying in the sun. For those customers willing to pay more for sturdier bricks, the Gypsies would stack the mud bricks in a triangular tent-shaped pile on a wooden base and fire them. Fire burned off their straw content and hardened the bricks. After completing the wall of the house, Gypsy masons wet the bricks and smoothed their surface with a fine, wet sand. Then, turning to the roof, they covered the beams with straw—rarely using tiles—and laid the straw compactly so that snow and rain would not leak inside and, instead, would flow to the ground and away from the house.

Gypsy women, often with a small child slung on their backs, supported their men by carrying the dried bricks to the wall under construction. In summer, most Gypsies (and many peasants) saved money by not wearing shoes; in winter, they wore inexpensive sandals (*bocskor* in Hungarian). Available for purchase at a local store, the sandals consisted of rubber squares with holes drilled along the sides for stringing the laces that were used to tie the sandals to the feet.

Tuesday was market day in Hadad. Peasants carried their produce to market in baskets balanced on the tops of their heads or under their arms.

Sitting on the ground in the town square, they laid out before them, on towels and blankets, their locally grown and processed food —milk, cheese, maize, wheat, meat, fruit, and spicy hamburger (*mititei* in Romanian). The women concentrated on selling fruits, vegetables, chickens with their legs tied together, and eggs.

Any Tuesday when I was not in school, I went to the market with my mother. She wore a simple skirt and blouse, and tied her hair up in a scarf. As we walked, the empty wooden basket she had made from tree branches bounced and swung on her right arm. Walking down the rows of peasant women selling produce, she would stop to examine the tomatoes, lettuce, and other vegetables. She stood before each vendor just long enough to examine the offerings and determine whether to purchase. Mother always bargained before buying.

"I give you fifty for it."

"No, I need sixty-five," the farmer would reply.

"Here is sixty, good-bye."

Once a month, another market located in the northernmost part of town offered live pigs, donkeys, horses, and cattle for sale. This monthly market featured serious bargaining over price. When the long negotiations finally concluded with an agreement, the parties slapped hands to seal the deal. These weekly and monthly markets were too exciting to miss, and I rarely did. Other than these market days, however, Hadad had little commercial activity, just its local retail trade.

News traveled by word of mouth in Hadad—not just during chance meetings, but also during gatherings before the town crier. Every Thursday, beating his drum with two sticks to attract attention, the town crier entered a corner of the market square in the center of town to make his announcements. People gathered quickly to learn about the latest official decrees and notices issued by the town clerk. The crier's tone was harsh and his news was often painful—it mostly involved taxes. Dressed in black boots and simple clothes, he was impressive. My friends and I followed him to his usual corner and listened intently to his every performance.

Funerals in Hadad were both solemn and public occasions. Six men carried the casket through the main street, first to the church and then to the nearby cemetery, while the immediate family and friends followed behind on foot. If the deceased was Reformed Protestant (Calvinist), which was usually the case—it was, after all, the town's majority religion—I felt comfortable attending funeral services because the minister of the Reformed Church was a family friend. I climbed the long, narrow ladder to the church steeple together with a young friend of mine whose father was the church caretaker and official bell-ringer. There we rang the bells announcing the funeral service before descending to the choir loft to join in the singing. Because my father was a local doctor and issued every death certificate, I usually knew who had died, often personally. Along with my friends and the other mourners, I followed the funeral processions to the gravesite, watched the lowering of the casket, and tossed earth into the grave.

To my recollection, Hadad had neither crime nor divorce; occasional carousing and gruffness constituted the only civil disturbances. Nevertheless, my father never went to bed without checking every door in our house to be sure it was locked. Dressed in pajamas and holding a kerosene lamp in one hand, he methodically made the rounds each night. (I inherited this habit from him, even though I now live in a similarly peaceful area of rural Connecticut.) In short, Hadad was a quiet pastoral community where multiple generations of families spent their entire lives. Its people worked, married, raised children, enjoyed some happy times, grew old, and then died, usually in the same house where they were born. Hadad was a little cocoon, largely uninformed about the momentous events taking place in Europe, since few people had a radio and town gossip focused on local concerns. Because Hadad was a remarkably peaceful place, I thought the outside world must be the same. Such was my perspective growing up in this isolated little northern Transylvania community—until the spring of 1944.

2.
Family Matters

Before turning to the traumatic events of 1944, I must introduce the reader to my family. My father, Morice Frenkel, was born in 1896 and raised in the city of Szamosujvar (Gherla), Transylvania. Szamosujvar is about twenty-eight miles north of Transylvania's capital city of Kolozsvar; both were part of Hungary from 1940 until the end of World War I. My father's father, Morton Frenkel, originally came from Germany. His mother, Cili (Leichter) Frenkel, came from Iclod, a small town near Szamosujvar in Transylvania. My father had two younger brothers, Max and Feri. Uncle Max and Uncle Feri both played a significant part in my postwar life in Romania (see Frenkel Family Tree).

My grandfather Morton Frenkel was a tailor who owned a small business in Szamosujvar that had six or seven apprentices. His shop was a single room located next to the kitchen of my grandparents' single-level house. Frequently, while attending middle school there in the early 1940s, I sat in Grandfather's shop watching his assistants at their sewing machines, stitching clothes. Grandfather Frenkel stood in front of them at a large table, cutting materials for peasant pants and jackets, following the layout of paper patterns.

My grandmother Cili Frenkel was generous, kind, and very religious—the most religious of my grandparents. Unfortunately for me, this limited the foods that she served at her home. First, it had to be kosher, and then, dairy and meat products had to be served in an orderly sequence. Also a hardworking businesswoman, Grandmother Frenkel sold textiles in her retail store, located about three quarters of a mile from their home. Each morning she set out on foot for the store with a basket on one arm containing her lunch. Once at the store, she sat patiently by the door waiting for the day's customers to arrive. Grandmother Frenkel had one employee, a girl in her twenties who helped my grandmother with customers and with chores at home. While living briefly with my Frenkel grandparents, I went to Grandmother's shop almost daily, helping her with customers by fetching rolls of textiles from the store shelves.

My mother Ida (Israel) Frenkel was born in 1901 and raised in Kolozsvar.

Her father, my grandfather Abraham Israel, was a shoemaker. I hardly knew Grandfather Israel, however, since he lived so far away from Hadad and died when I was less than ten years old. I never knew my grandmother Mariska Israel, who died before I was born. My mother was the oldest of the six Israel children. Her siblings included my uncles David, Ernest (Laicsi), and Eugene, and my aunts Magda and Nelli. My three uncles and my aunt Nelli emigrated from Romania to the United States in the 1930s when I was one year old. The three uncles on my mother's side and my aunt Nellie's son Danny played a significant role in my later life in America. Grandfather Israel remarried after his first wife's death and had another son by his second wife, my uncle Ervin, who was about the age of my older brother, Gabriel. After Grandfather Israel died, his widow (whose first name I cannot remember) lived together with Aunt Magda and Uncle Ervin in Kolozsvar. Gabriel moved in with them while attending gymnasium in Kolozsvar.

When World War I broke out in August 1914, my father was eighteen. Drafted into the Austro-Hungarian Army, he was stationed on the Italian front and even suffered a slight wound there. Father told me about his harrowing wartime experience enduring artillery bombardments and poison-gas attacks. His stories made me curious about the war, and I pored over a neighbor's many war books, with their graphic pictures of cannon fire, trench warfare, and grimy soldiers with gas masks. Father's military service took him throughout southern Europe and increased his fluency in German.

After the war, Father initially attended medical school in Budapest, Hungary, but later finished his medical studies in Kolozsvar. There he met and married my mother in 1923. Because of widespread anti-Semitism, my father had few professional opportunities in hospitals and medical facilities anywhere in Hungary. So he accepted a state position as a general practitioner—first in a town near Arad, Romania (where Gabriel was born), and subsequently in Hadad. He was a circuit doctor (*kor orvos* in Hungarian), the only medical doctor serving Hadad and its eighteen to twenty neighboring towns. As the state medical doctor and pathologist for our area, Father provided medical services for the poor, administered immunization shots to schoolchildren, and issued death certificates. In addition to his government-appointed medical position, Father also saw

Frenkel Family Tree

Father's Family

Morton */Clii Frenkel *

Max/Sidona   +   Max/Margo   Feri/Piri

Morice *

Judith/George   Gabriel/Ronnie   Eddie   Nathan   Agi   Erica

Robert   Thomas   Barbara   Cynthia   Robin   Rachel   Avi   Michael

Mother's Family

Adolf/Mariska Israel + ?

Ida *   Magda *   Ervin *

Nellie+/ David Weitzner   David+/ Helen Ince   Daniel/Tilly   Naomi/Clifford Hart   Earnest+/ Helen Ince   Eugene+/ Erna Ince

David   Victor/Michelle/ Nadine   Rebecca   Bobby   Eugene   David/Donna   Katherene   Susan/Martin Flicker

Jake   Alex   Daryl   Kristen   Heather

Morice * Ida Frenkel *

Gabriel/Naomi   Paul/Rita (Maduro)

David   Deborah   Victoria (Tori)/ Tom Beier   Nicholas (Nick)/ Nanci

Isabel   Suzanna   Theo   Simon   Oliver   Logan

Note: * Murdered in the Holocaust
         + Left Transylvania for the US in 1930

23

private patients to supplement his state income. Although Father stood at the top of the civic and economic ladder in Hadad, he seemed constantly beset by economic worries.

My mother was educated at the Marianum, a prominent Roman Catholic gymnasium (middle school) located along the main street in Kolozsvar between the railroad station and King Matthias Square. Mother remained intellectually curious and well-read even as a busy housewife and attentive mother of two young boys. She loved music and sang popular Hungarian peasant songs while working in the kitchen. In addition to cooking all our meals, she spent much of every day preparing and bottling various preserves to carry us throughout the year, especially during the harsh winter.

I particularly liked her plum marmalade, or *lekvar*. To make lekvar, she boiled pitted fresh plums in a huge, unique five- to ten-gallon copper kettle. The kettle rested on a wood fire submerged in a hole in the ground dug outside the kitchen specifically for this purpose. Using a long wooden spoon, she and our maid took turns stirring the boiling pot of plums until they disintegrated and concentrated into a thick liquid. Then she stored the finished marmalade in small, sterilized jars. A typical Hungarian delicacy, lekvar was indescribably delicious, especially when spread on fresh homemade bread.

Every Friday, Mother baked bread in an outdoor oven close to our fence line, but located in the yard of our neighbors, the Richters. The prior day, our maid prepared the dough and stored it overnight to ferment in a large wooden tub covered tightly with a towel. In the morning, the maid cut the dough into smaller pieces, pressed them flat, and slid them into the oven on a wooden pallet. As soon as the baked bread emerged from the oven, my mother gave each of us a large, warm slice covered with butter. Nothing then or since has tasted more scrumptious to me.

We made our butter from cream placed inside a large jar and shaken by everyone in turn until it thickened. Next we removed the heavy cream from the jar, discarded the whey, and whipped the cream until it became butter. Milk from local cows, homemade butter, and home-baked bread made a daily appearance in homes like ours throughout Hadad.

Chicken was our primary source of protein. Mother purchased chickens at the local market, and I took them to the Hebrew teacher, or *schachter*, who was also the ritual slaughterer, to have them killed. In the backyard of the synagogue, the schachter cut off the chicken's head. I watched in distress as the chicken ran around headless until it collapsed. The schachter cut open and examined the stomach to assure it was kosher. Then he returned the chicken to me to take home for roasting or boiling before eating.

In the late afternoon after school let out, Mother always had dinner waiting for me. It was a small affair with bread, butter, and jam, or alternatively, cornbread. Our breakfast also was modest, just cornmeal polenta with milk. Cornmeal was the staple of the Transylvanian diet. Our principal meal of the day was noontime lunch, which consisted of soup, a piece of heavy rye bread, and chicken. Lunch was never big enough, however, to deter me from returning home in midafternoon for coffee and cake, and on Fridays for warm, freshly baked bread with butter.

Aside from the kosher chicken, my family was not demonstrably religious and did not strictly observe kosher. We did attend services at the synagogue on Saturdays and high holy days, but we did not wear the dark religious clothes, yarmulkes, or devices that distinguished most of the other Jews in Hadad. Occasionally we snacked on strips of pork cut from the side of a pig that Father smoked inside the chimney. As secular Jews, we were more readily accepted in town by the Christian majority. Also, as the sole doctor in town, my father received a measure of respect from everyone.

My parents rarely took trips out of town, except to visit family in Szamosujvar or Kolozsvar. On one occasion, however, they traveled to Budapest. There they attended the theater and the circus, even enjoyed a Turkish bath, and returned home with many stories. My parents never entertained at home, as we do in the United States. The houses in Hadad were too small for this purpose. Instead, our social life consisted primarily of shopping in the market and attending the synagogue, where we met with friends. The one exception was a German family, the Aichelins. When Gabriel and I were small, Mother befriended and frequently visited Mrs. Aichelin, wife of the Lutheran minister. Gabriel and I often accompanied

Mother on these visits and played with the Aichelins' two small daughters, who were our ages.

Gabriel was four years and six months older than me—he was born on January 22, 1925, and I on July 24, 1929. I was known as *Öcsi*, or "little brother." Upon returning home to Hadad after my birth in Kolozsvar, Mother presented me to Gabriel as a complete surprise. Gabriel later told me of his anger toward our parents for failing to prepare him for my arrival. He felt that I had usurped his place of primacy. Because of our age difference, Gabriel and I had different friends, and we rarely spent time together.

Gabriel was independent and studious. On visits home from school out of town, he spent endless hours reclining on a canvas-covered chair, reading alone beneath the low-hanging branches of the spruce trees near the Banfi property. From a very young age, Gabriel loved opera, and in Munich after the war he became an avid operagoer. Whereas my interests tended toward nature and the outdoors, Gabriel's lay exclusively in academics and intellectual pursuits. We did share one common interest, however: collecting stamps. Each of us had his own stamp album made from desk calendars that the Bayer Company gave my father annually to promote its pharmaceutical products.

Because Hadad offered school only from kindergarten through approximately grade five, Gabriel left Hadad at age eleven to pursue his upper-level schooling in Zilai (Zalau), about twenty-five miles south and equidistant between Hadad and Kolozsvar. My mother had relatives in Zilai with whom Gabriel lived while attending school there. After Zilai, Gabriel moved to Kolozsvar, where he attended a Jewish high school with stringent academic standards. There Gabriel displayed exceptional ability in mathematics and excelled in all his subjects, especially German and French. Except for summer vacations, Gabriel lived away from Hadad for most of the year from the time I turned six years of age—the eight years (1936–44) before our deportation. When the Nazis occupied Hungary in the spring of 1944, Gabriel returned home from Kolozsvar to be with the family.

Father's medical office consisted of two adjacent rooms located either within or next to our home (its precise location differed with each home).

In one room he saw patients, and in the other he housed his x-ray machine. To generate the electric power for the x-ray machine, Father had to crank up a gasoline motor by hand. He kept this motor in a nearby building. Before operating the x-ray machine, he donned a pair of long heavy gloves and a heavy lead-filled apron, which covered him from shoulders to knees. He took great pride in this modern German diagnostic tool never before seen in rural Transylvania.

During the 1930s and 40s, very sick patients expected their doctor to see them at home because of the seriousness of their condition, the difficulties of travel, and the lack of a local hospital. Thus, in addition to treating patients at his home office, my father made regular rounds to patients' homes, traveling on foot or horseback, or by horse-drawn carriage, regardless of the distance or weather conditions. From about age eight, I accompanied Father during his school visits to immunize children and his home visits to attend bedridden patients. The house calls were solemn occasions. Upon our arrival, the patient's mother or spouse greeted us at the doorstep and led us down a hallway or through a kitchen to the main room or bedroom where the patient was resting. As we approached, we often heard the patient moaning in pain or discomfort and usually found him or her dressed warmly in a long nightgown and lying under a large down bedcover.

Following his standard practice during house calls, my father checked the patient's temperature; inspected his or her mouth, ears, and eyes; and listened with a stethoscope at various spots on the patient's upper body. He then placed his palm on the patient's torso, while tapping it with the knuckles of his other hand. He asked pertinent questions of the patient, or a relative if the patient could not answer. Throughout his examination, family members stood around the bed quietly observing the process and anxiously awaiting Father's diagnosis. After a brief period of silent reflection, Father would report his findings, write out a prescription on a notepad, and relay his instructions for patient care. The family asked polite questions concerning the patient's prospects and, as Father replied, they attended as much to his tone as to his words. Sometimes Father's report on the patient's condition would relieve everyone's anxiety; other times, his report was more serious and upsetting. But he always offered encouragement and hope.

Occasionally a female patient was deemed "hysterical"—psychologically troubled rather than physically ill. In this case, Father would write out a bogus prescription in a code understood only by him and the pharmacist. Every patient expected to receive a prescription, whether needed or not, in order to feel properly treated. For such a "sick" person, Father would write "penis erectus," alerting the pharmacist to fill a bottle with some placebo. Of course, seriously ill patients might require hospitalization, which was available only in a distant city, like Kolozsvar. In such cases, Father would arrange for a special horse-drawn carriage containing a bed with sheets, pillows, and down covers. The carriage transported the patient to the nearest train station at Szilagy Cseh, a one- to two-hour trip. From there, the patient went by train to a hospital in Kolozsvar, another four hours away.

I still remember my own experience at age nine when I came down with septicemia, a bacterial infection in the bloodstream that even today can be fatal. Lying on a straw bed in the horse-drawn carriage on the way to the Szilagy Cseh train station, en route to the hospital in Kolozsvar for treatment, I remember passing by Hadad Cemetery with its dirt mounds and gravestones. I wondered if I would ever return home alive.

The only patients of Father's whom I disliked watching during treatment were those with toothaches. My father also served as the dentist, so patients came to him with dental problems that sometimes required extractions. Since anesthesia was unavailable, Father's trick was to pull out the tooth with his special pliers in one quick motion. Some teeth stubbornly resisted this technique, however, and required prolonged loosening. The patient's resulting pain was excruciating and his screams deafening. Consequently, when a patient needed a tooth pulled, I promptly left Father's office and remained out of earshot. Even before the patient arrived, I knew what to expect simply by observing the instruments that Father was sterilizing in a boiling pot or storing inside a covered stainless-steel urn. When I saw the sterilized pliers, I headed out—a single experience watching a tooth being pulled was quite enough.

As payment for his private medical services, either in his office or on house calls, Father often received produce. This might include cherries, berries, apples, plums, walnuts, chestnuts, potatoes, corn, tomatoes, grapes, and even chickens. Several baskets in our kitchen and living room/ bedroom overflowed with such payments in-kind—at best, an inexact return for services rendered. Sometimes a patient would call out from our front yard, "Sir doctor, I am bringing you something." My father or mother answered from the kitchen, hurried outside to investigate, and returned with a basket or two of seasonal vegetables and fruits. "Here it is, come and taste it," my mother would announce to me. We kept the fruits in baskets and enjoyed them over several days, a visible reward for Father's hard work.

Father's medical practice provided the means for a reasonable lifestyle, but he was always short of money. Father was well-respected and enjoyed a good medical practice, so most people placed us high upon the social ladder. Still, we struggled to make ends meet. It troubled me to hear my parents in constant distress over our finances. Seeing how hard my father worked for such a modest income, I developed an urge to contribute to the family coffers. So I opened a savings account at the local post office (Hadad contained no banks). When Father began buying cows and grain for speculation, I knew that we were living dangerously on the edge of our income. Yet I often wonder where Father obtained the funds to buy a second house in Szamosujvar when I went to gymnasium there in 1940, if not from his speculative ventures.

One night a man was found dead in the field of a neighboring town. As state pathologist, Father had to perform an autopsy to determine the cause of death. The neighboring town had no facility designated or suitable for such a purpose, and so an issue arose about exactly where Father should perform the autopsy. Someone among the many townsfolk who came to view the body suggested that he perform the autopsy inside the cemetery, right next to the grave. Father agreed. No sooner had they dug the grave in the hillside cemetery than a second question arose about where to place the body for the autopsy. Father needed a table or other surface to move around in order to do his work. Once again, someone proposed a solution: remove the cemetery gate from its hinges and support it on rocks beside the grave. So there, on the cemetery gate balanced on rocks next to the gravesite, Father performed a very public autopsy on the naked corpse.

People gathered round as Father began to dissect the corpse. He removed and weighed the organs one by one, examined each body part in detail, cut open the skull to weigh the brain, and then placed each organ into a bag. Father impressed upon everyone not to touch any body parts because they were poisonous and potentially lethal. As the autopsy progressed, public curiosity slowly turned to revulsion. Upon completing the autopsy, Father replaced the organs within the body cavity and sewed up the chest with needle and thread. Then he signaled for the body to be placed into a rectangular box that served as a casket and to be lowered into the grave. Throughout the process, Father wore rubber gloves, which he threw into the grave along with everything else that came into contact with the corpse—the deceased's clothing, my father's apron, and the cemetery gate. Since the autopsy revealed no violence, Father concluded that the man died from natural causes, probably a lethal combination of stress and alcohol.

The respect given my father as the doctor for Hadad and its surrounding communities gave me and my family a feeling of status and security throughout my childhood. I was proud to see my father sought out for his medical opinion, and I remained inspired all my life by his professional dedication. He responded to patients' needs at any hour of the day or night and in all kinds of weather. Furthermore, Father radiated genuine empathy for all his patients—even those imagining an illness and requesting a prescription, or fearing the military draft and seeking a doctor's waiver. In the latter case, his motivation was humanitarian rather than political, since he maintained respect for Germany because of its alignment with the Austro-Hungarian Empire during World War I.

Despite the respect accorded me as the doctor's son, I never wanted to be a medical doctor. My father worked extremely hard, whether traveling away from home on distant medical calls or sitting at his desk in the corner of our living room/bedroom immersed in heavy paperwork. I still picture him pulling his gray hair in frustration over the burdens of completing official medical reports and of making financial ends meet.

In Hadad, we lived in three different homes (see Map 3). From my birth until I was eight (1929–1937), we lived in a white single-family house located on a side road in the lower part of town. By far the nicest of our three homes, it had privacy, several rooms, a porch, and a large garden at the side of the house facing the road out front. Like other homes in Hadad, it had no electricity or running water, and it lacked an attic. But the house had a small basement in which we stored wine and food, including Mother's great fruit preserves. Our single-level living space had typical mud-brick walls, which were painted white inside and out. From the swing on our front porch in the summer, we could view Mother's garden, planted thick with vegetables, berries, and tomatoes (my personal favorite), all hidden from the road behind a high hedge. After becoming sick one day from overeating tomatoes, I avoided the garden for a while. Still, I picked berries when they ripened as a present for Mother. Every Friday, a peasant woman came to assist Mother. The woman scrubbed the floors, carried the wood and water into the house, churned the cream into butter, and washed the clothes and hung them on the line to dry.

Our first home had only one disadvantage, which ultimately proved unacceptable to Father: its location. Because the roads in Hadad were notoriously bad—strewn with stones and caked with mud or snow during three seasons—patients had great difficulty most days descending the slippery road to Father's home office. Thus, when Count Banfi offered an apartment in one of his courtyard buildings in exchange for medical services to his family, Father readily accepted. So, in 1937, having just turned eight, I moved in among Magyar royalty—or so the Hungarian aristocrats were called.

Banfi Castle had an elegant façade, with an overhead panel in the vestibule bearing some ancient Latin inscription never translated into Hungarian for me (see photograph). Rose beds surrounded the castle, and two large pine trees marked the front entrance. About fifty feet from the castle in the lower garden was a deep, dry well with a mysterious and notorious past. According to local lore, Count Dracula had cast his victims into this well, where they were impaled on the points of scythes as they landed at the bottom.

From 1937 to 1943, when I was between the ages of eight and thirteen, we lived in one section of a three-sided building that formed the courtyard of the castle. Our modest kitchen was separated from Count Banfi's grand kitchen by a single wall. During the day, servants paraded from the kitchen to the castle, carrying meals prepared for the count and his family to enjoy in their elegant dining room. Our kitchen contained a closet, a stove, a table, and some chairs. A doorway divided the kitchen from our living room/bedroom, which constituted one large space. The apartment was comfortable yet spare. The mud stove in our kitchen and the terra-cotta stove in our bedroom heated the entire place. Every fall, a cattle-drawn wagon delivered long pieces of wood to the castle courtyard. For a small fee, we hired day laborers to chop and stack enough wood to last us through the long winter.

The castle's nearest source of drinking water was about one mile away, down a long path through the forest at the bottom of a hill. There, well water poured out of a steel pipe. Every day for many years, our maid—limping along the way on her congenitally bad foot—carried two buckets of water up this steep path to our house. Finally, someone thought of loading a barrel onto a two-wheel cart, filling the barrel at the well, and hitching a donkey to the cart to haul it back up the hill. All the maid needed to do was coax the donkey along with grass and oats. The donkey was none too fond of its strenuous new assignment, and one day it exacted revenge on me. As I held its halter during the long climb, the donkey bit one of my fingers and gave me a painful kick.

We kept the drinking water drawn from the well in two large buckets covered with lids and placed in the kitchen on a low stool for easy access. On top of one lid rested a metal drinking cup. Winter snow sometimes relieved us of the long trips to the well, as occasionally we collected and melted it in pots on our kitchen stove. The Banfis, by contrast, did not have to contend with this manual system. They received their drinking water via gravity flow from an old concrete reservoir on the hill above the castle. A steam engine pumped the same well water through an underground pipe up the hill to the reservoir. From there, the water flowed by pipe into the tap faucets in the castle's kitchen.

The building in the courtyard directly opposite our apartment was empty, except for a single room that contained the outhouse (toilet). Even though we had to walk across the courtyard to relieve ourselves, we felt privileged to have the toilet on a wooden deck inside a room rather than out in the open. Most people in town had only a small wooden shed over a hole in the ground. This was the case with our first home. Of course, our toilet at the castle had no running water and could not be flushed. Also, there was no toilet paper—we used surplus paper from my father's office. Once, Father accidentally dropped his stethoscope into the toilet hole. This kept him busy for hours until he retrieved it using two long sticks. At night, we used old-fashioned chamber pots, which we carried across the courtyard each morning—carefully and at arm's length—to empty into the toilet. Even in Banfi Castle, our life was still fairly primitive by today's standards.

A large iron gate at the entrance to the Banfi courtyard marked it as a private residence, even though the gate always remained open. There were no other houses in the immediate vicinity of the castle, except for the police station. It was tucked off in the woods across the street from the castle and hidden from the main road. What I valued most about the estate was the large inventory of milking cows, the several breeding bulls used to maintain the herd, and the Lipizzaner, Arabian, and other breeds of horses.

Unlike the quiet neighborhood of our prior house, Banfi Castle was a beehive of farming activity. In addition, Magyar aristocrats periodically arrived from distant towns in their chauffeur-driven automobiles to hunt boar and pheasants on the count's estate. I stared in wonderment at these strange intermittent visitors, who looked and spoke like beings from another world.

In 1943, for reasons I never understood, we left our home in the Banfi courtyard after six years there and moved into our third house, located in the town center. This was a two-room apartment situated on the main road east of Banfi Castle, between the market square and the town hall. Across the road from this house, about fifty feet away and below a small embankment, stood Hadad's second castle, built in the period from 1790 to 1810. By comparison with the Banfi estate farther up the hill and off to the west, the Degenfeld estate appeared dormant: it had no herds of animals, no lands under cultivation, and no one living inside its high surrounding wall except for the caretaker and his family. They lived next to the castle in a small house. Degenfeld Castle had no furnishings, and its wine cellar had no wine. The estate manager lived about one quarter mile from the castle, near a barn that housed several stallions, which provided one of the few signs of life on the estate.

We rented our third apartment from a Jewish couple who occupied a rear apartment in the same house. Our landlord owned a small bar located in a separate building within the courtyard next to our house. The bar had a convenient street entrance facing the market square. Customers were mainly Hungarian and Romanian peasants visiting town on Tuesday for market day. They drank wine and plum brandy while singing to Gypsy violin music. Late in the evening, after the market and bar had closed, I often found some out-of-town patrons of either this or the town's one other tavern lying asleep in a roadside ditch, unable to make their long way home. Upon discovering them lying there, the police dragged the drunks off to a cell in the basement of the police station until they sobered up.

The police station was also the police chief's home. Since the chief's son was my friend, I often visited his home on Wednesday mornings following market day. Peering into his basement window, I observed the disheveled drunks groaning in their morning-after stupor. Usually from some neighboring town, these incarcerated peasants had come from too far away for the Hadad police to usher them home at night. Consequently, locking them up was probably in their best interest. Although they never appeared to be self-conscious about their humiliating condition, I always felt sorry and embarrassed for them. Hadad residents, however, must have accepted this periodic drunkenness, since no one ever bothered to chastise the drunks. Apparently their conduct was considered a price of doing business. After all, these peasants generally were their good customers. The next day, after the peasants had sobered up, the police chief routinely released them to travel home on their own.

Our third home was only about a hundred yards away from Hadad's principal well, located in the town center not far from the main road. Our maid used this well daily to fetch two full buckets of water, stopping periodically along the way home to rest from the strain of carrying such a heavy weight. Like the other townspeople, we used this well water not just for drinking but also for cooking, washing clothes, and the occasional bath. During winter, the water that spilled around the well quickly turned to ice, which was dangerously slick and a serious hazard.

Next to the well was a large, long wooden trough used daily to water horses and cattle. Farmers would herd ten to twenty of their animals into the town center to drink from the trough. When several groups of animals arrived simultaneously, fights broke out among them, with the beasts kicking and biting one another as they struggled for a place at the trough. Filling the animal trough from the well was dangerous and took considerable skill. It required balancing a long horizontal pole set on top of a vertical beam planted firmly into the ground. A bucket tethered to one end of the pole was offset by a huge rock fastened to the other end. Manipulating the pole, particularly in winter while standing on solid ice, was no job for the fainthearted.

Growing up in Hadad, I admired my father's dedicated professionalism and well-earned respect within the community. But I also hoped one day to live comfortably without his constant financial worries. Managing a farm like the Banfis', I thought, might provide the answer. I came to this conclusion gradually after befriending two older Hungarians who taught me a lot about farming: Mihaly Antal, Count Banfi's horse caretaker (and a World War I veteran of the Austro-Hungarian Army, like my father), and Moses Adorjan, the count's estate manager. I met them after moving into our apartment in the Banfi courtyard, and I came to respect both men as exemplars. In time, I learned their jobs much better than I understood my father's, and I owe them a great debt of gratitude for my lifelong interest in agriculture.

3.
Young and Innocent

Growing up, I loved everything about Hadad—its farms, its fields, its forests, its seasons, its weather, and its friendliness. The days were never long enough, and Hadad life absorbed my every waking minute. I always wanted to squeeze in just one more activity: to witness the nightly parade of cows and pigs as they returned home from pasture; to admire the daylong pecking of the chickens as they cleaned yards of fallen seeds; to gallop another lap on horseback around the Degenfeld courtyard; to stuff my pockets with the warm, freshly shelled sunflower seeds at the mill; or to gather under my shirt a few cherries, peaches, or plums from the orchard for the walk home. Of course, I had my home chores too: picking fruits and berries from the trees and bushes in our garden; folding and carrying in the dried clothes from the outdoor clothesline; and carrying armloads of wood into the house for our stoves. When not attending school or doing home chores, I was exploring the town and its surrounding countryside. Every day was an adventure.

From about age five, while living in our first home, I began exploring the town, and my parents began to worry about me. They decided to intervene—I had to be home by dark. If I was not home by then, Father would come looking for me at the neighbors' homes, murmuring his usual recriminations as we walked home together. "Didn't I tell you to be at home early, hmm? Answer me!"

"Yes, I know, but I forgot."

"So, here," and he tugged gently on my earlobe. A scolding and ear-tugging were the worst punishments my father ever administered.

At age eight, when we moved into the Banfi courtyard apartment, my enthusiasm for Hadad's farm life quickened. The middle building of the courtyard, directly opposite the castle, housed a barn where the count sheltered about four purebred Arabian horses. These Arabians pulled the Banfi family carriage to and from the Szilagy Cseh train station. Mihaly Antal was Count Banfi's horse caretaker and coach driver. I called him Mihaly Bacsi, or Uncle Mihaly (pronounced "*Me* hi"). When driving the horse carriage up to the castle door to pick up passengers for a trip, Uncle Mihaly took special pride in aligning the carriage wheels with the castle steps, placing it exactly between the two tall pine trees across the driveway and just opposite the castle door. Uncle Mihaly was always meticulously dressed, his boots well-shined, and his white peasant shirt carefully buttoned at the neck.

Uncle Mihaly lived with his wife and numerous children in a small two-room house below the castle at the bottom of the hill, near the well. His two older boys and I often played together in the fields by their home. Every day I saw their mother carrying buckets of water from the well to wash the family clothes alongside their house. She always seemed to be pregnant and gave birth to one child after another. Large families like Mihaly's were unusual in Hadad; the norm was at most three children. Since people in Hadad were generally uneducated, poor, and lacking any source of income besides farming, large families posed an almost insurmountable economic burden. I often wondered how Uncle Mihaly's large family could make do on his small income from the Banfi estate, and how they all fit into their tiny home.

Along the same middle wing of the Banfi courtyard that contained the horse stalls was a separate cow barn. In that barn, I first saw cows milked by hand. I watched and listened as spurts of milk shot into the bucket placed beneath the milkmaid's hands as she tugged and squeezed the cow's teats. Immediately after milking the cow, she took the buckets of warm milk directly into the kitchen and boiled it. To service these cows, the count owned a few large bulls, which he kept in a building at a safe distance behind the cow barn and accessible only from outside the courtyard.

While the house staff tended the horses and cows housed in the courtyard, peasant farmers looked after the sheep and pigs housed in a separate barn located at some distance from the castle. In yet another remote barn, peasants bagged wheat, sunflowers, and grain for delivery to the nearby flour mill. They also spread manure with pitchforks or shovels, and tossed bales of hay onto great piles. Everything was done by hand; their work was repetitive, messy, and strenuous.

I met Moses Adorjan, the Banfi estate manager, soon after we moved to the castle. On my days off from school I frequently accompanied him on his routine, daylong trips to inspect the count's sprawling farmland. Then in his mid-thirties, Moses had a kindly round face but a professional demeanor. He did not dress in peasant clothing. Instead, he wore a colored necktie, polished boots, and a green hunting hat with feathers. Moses carried a horsewhip as a formality. While making the rounds, I sat next to him on the front seat of his carriage and even drove the horses. I found it quite a challenge to maintain the horses' pace while holding the reins in one hand and the horsewhip in the other. During our trips we inspected the sheep and pig farms and the vast fields of grain, and we talked to the farmworkers about their pressing concerns. Often we carried home with us a bag of fruit and a large five- to ten-pound round of ripe cheese. These estate tours with Moses were fun but exhausting. Upon returning home at nightfall, I was ready for bed.

When not inspecting the farms with Moses, I was caring for the horses with Uncle Mihaly. Many days, I joined him between five and six a.m. to assist in feeding hay and oats to the horses. Mihaly taught me how to maintain and repair the horse carts, harnesses, saddles, and blankets. I watched him breeding the horses and cattle and admired the stallions' drive and the mares' submissiveness. Uncle Mihaly had a unique process for brushing the count's Lipizzaner and Arabian horses, and after grooming a horse, he'd pound dust out from the brush on the barn floor outside the stall to form the count's crown. One evening, as I was about to leave for home, the count walked into the barn carrying a basket of fruit on his arm. Approaching me, he said, "You have done a terrific job, and this is your payment." I could not wait to get home to show my parents that I had begun to earn a living.

During the September harvest season, I picked grapes in the Banfi vineyard, carried the loaded baskets to the vine shed, and dumped my loads into the winepress. Two men cranked the large handle of the press's screw that squeezed out the juice. When the process of compressing the grapes bogged down, these workers removed their shoes, climbed into the press, and trampled the grapes with their bare feet. They poured the grape juice into large wooden barrels and hauled the barrels into the Banfi wine cellar located just beneath the castle. Laid out in long rows, these wooden barrels filled the entire floor of the cellar.

Periodically, my friends and I slipped into the long corridor leading to the count's wine cellar to sample his latest vintage. Each wine barrel had its own convenient front spigot from which we poured the wine into a bucket. Passing the bucket among us, each one in turn tilted it above his head to pour out the *vin nouveau*. The experience was less a wine tasting than a communal shower, drenching our pants and shirts. Despite the telltale stains and smell on our clothing, however, we managed to conceal this imbibing from our parents.

Growing up, my best friend was Joska Richter, a Hungarian boy of German-Swabian extraction. One day he and I tried to create our own press, grinding some wild, black, and inedible berries that we stripped from nearby bushes and forced through a pipe with a makeshift screw. This process produced a tasteless and useless, blue-black, gooey mush—not the tasty jam that we had anticipated. Undeterred by the unsuitability of this concoction as processed jam, we reconceived it as a new medicine or industrial lubricant. In addition to our berry-processing activity, Joska and I tried parachuting. Holding an umbrella overhead, we jumped down fifteen to twenty feet from the top of hay bales stacked inside a barn. As paratroopers buffeted by crosswinds and updrafts, we came to expect the inevitable hard landings. Joska was smart but had a hearing impairment. This required that we shout at one another, which added to our racket.

At Joska's house, I watched his parents slaughter one of their pigs, a fascinating though grim affair. The entire ritual lasted a day or two, as the live animal transitioned into ham, bacon, sausage, and other delicacies. It began with a screaming pig being driven to a spot in the yard covered lightly with hay. Both parents, usually with the aid of a third person, wrestled the animal to the ground while one of them cut its jugular with a knife. As the blood came oozing out, someone quickly placed a pot under the pig's neck to save the blood for use in making sausages. The pig's screaming persisted for a while and then slowly faded to a groan as it died. At this point, they covered the carcass with dry straw and ignited the straw to burn off the pig's hair. When the fire died out, someone poured hot water over the animal while the others scraped and shaved its skin with sharp knives to clean off the burned hair. Gradually my sadness over the pig's death subsided, and I came to recognize the animal only as food. Following the slaughter, someone usually handed me a piece of singed tail or ear to chew on. It was a delicacy.

In the summer of 1941, the Hungarian Army marched east through Hadad. This occurred approximately one year after northern Transylvania became Hungarian, and shortly after Germany's invasion of Russia that June. Like all the other Hadad children, Joska and I felt a rush of excitement as the army headed down the main street and passed by my house in the Banfi estate. I ran to greet the passing soldiers and climbed aboard the military wagons and artillery pieces. They were all horse-drawn—not a single motorized vehicle among them. What a thrill it was for me as a young boy to see an army marching off to war, too young at the time to understand the ominous import of this martial pomp and splendor.

I asked the passing soldiers, "Where are you going?"

"We cannot tell you."

I followed up with, "Where do you sleep?"

"In the field," they replied.

So, from my very first encounter with the Hungarian Army, I learned that military affairs were secret, not to be shared with the civilian population.

Given the absence of newspapers, we learned little about the war except for what we could pick up on Father's radio. An external battery powered the radio, which stood on his desk in our bedroom. Even radio news was limited, however, consisting largely of broadcasts by Hungarian fascists and speeches by Hitler in German. Since Father spoke German, he listened intently and with increasing alarm to Hitler's frequent rants about the Jews, which he translated and summarized for Mother and me. Although Hitler's views grew more threatening toward the Jews, we discounted their import for us, given Father's World War I service in the Austro-Hungarian Army and his status in the local community.

Consequently, we had little idea of their dire personal implications for us. In remote Hadad, we had no contact with the larger Jewish community in Hungary and received no word-of-mouth news about the mortal danger to European Jews. The war itself seemed safely distant from us.

Count Banfi had two sons, Tomas and Bella, who were my friends. They periodically ventured into the castle courtyard to play with me, always accompanied by their chaperone, a German lady. We might ride a donkey or a horse in the courtyard or even play inside their palatial residence. They had a large trove of toys unlike anything I had ever seen or even dreamed of. Tomas and Bella never ventured into town or played with peasant children, whom they no doubt considered below their social rank. The aristocratic life, however, was too rarefied and stifling for me. After a while in their company I soon lost interest and sidled off to see Uncle Mihaly and his horses or to visit my other friends in town. Nevertheless, I felt comfortable on the count's estate. The count seemed to like me and I respected him.

In 1943, when I was thirteen, we left the Banfi courtyard to occupy our third home on the main street, and I found myself living opposite the Degenfeld estate. The Degenfeld caretaker was a nice, hardworking old man who lived in a small wooden house on the property with his wife, a son my age, and two beautiful daughters. I was close friends with the entire family and took great delight when my good friend Moses Adorjan married one of his daughters.

The caretaker not only looked after the Degenfeld estate but also carried heavy buckets of slop to his pigs in the yard and grain to his chickens in their cages behind the house. The strain of work showed on his body and face. His wife also worked continuously around the house, stirring the pots of food on the stove, washing clothes by hand, and hanging them on the clotheslines stretched among trees in the yard. They frequently invited me to eat with them in their combination kitchen/living room, usually an offering of fruit and something made from corn.

I was friends with their son, who was frail, sickly, and confined by his health to the courtyard. The caretaker's son and I liked to explore the estate, which was full of mysterious unused chambers. No one ever entered the dark, forbidding basement closed off by a rusty iron gate or the damp underground tunnel that probably served as a wine cellar in the 1790s when the estate was built. We decided to steer clear of them too. Instead, given his son's poor state of health, we confined our activity mostly to playing chess.

The courtyard served as the corral for the caretaker's large horse. I learned to ride his horse bareback, with one hand holding its mane and the other maneuvering the guiding rope tied around its muzzle. After the horse and I became comfortable with each other, we galloped among the trees, chased by the caretaker's large white dog. Even sliding from side to side on the horse's back, I still felt safe because a high concrete wall surrounded the estate and kept the horse from dashing off the property into the streets and fields.

Outside its high walls, but still within the estate and not far from the caretaker's house, was the residence of the estate's general manager. The residence also served as his office, and contained a desk, a chair, a closet, and several shelves where he maintained his records. Periodically I worked for him, helping to fill out work records. Sitting on a chair at his desk, I entered on payroll timesheets the number of hours spent by workers who looked after the few animals on the estate. On one occasion, he took me inside the castle to see its many unfurnished formal rooms with their high ceilings, mirrors, finished floors, and painted walls. Sadly, Degenfeld Castle remained unoccupied.

When not exploring farms (or in school), I visited Hadad's various skilled tradesmen. The shoemaker's shop was near our third home, located on the main street. Strewn all about his workbench and shop floor were pieces of leather, old shoes, and miscellaneous debris. Sitting on a low stool beside the shoemaker's workbench, I watched him bend over his work with intense focus. He stitched and nailed the leather and attached the sole to the shoe, all without using any machine. Once when I ordered a pair of shoes from the cobbler, he had me hold the leather in place above the sole. "Come on, hold it fast," he said. Then he took one of several nails from between his lips and hammered the leather into place before trimming it to the shape of the sole. I have never forgotten the wonderful smell of leather that permeated his shop. He worked hard, with meticulous care, but earned very little from making shoes for the families in town.

In addition to the shoemaker, who was Jewish, I regularly called upon the Hadad tailor, who also was Jewish. He made simple work clothes, suits to order, and ornamental national-style clothes for Hadad's peasant population. Using cloth that Mother picked out for my suits, the tailor pieced together the parts and fitted them to me over several visits until the suit looked perfect. (For years after coming to America, I felt strange buying ready-made shoes and suits in department stores, although I was relieved at not having to return suits for additional fittings.) Because Hadad had its own tailor and cobbler, my family rarely bought clothes and shoes in any of the larger cities. Traveling to cities like Szamosujvar or Kolozsvar took a full day each way by horse cart and train. Since Hadad's tailor and shoemaker made quality goods, they served us just fine. Next to being a farm manager, I preferred the cobbler's and the tailor's professions.

Among the various local trades, the barber seemed to have it best. He had his own clean indoor working space with chairs and mirrors. He not only cut my hair regularly, but I saw him almost daily. I needed to cross the street directly in front of his barbershop in order to get anywhere west of town. The barber also owned the town's only bicycle, which he parked safely inside his shop behind the barber chair. He cared for the bicycle like some precious family heirloom. As a big favor, since I was such a valued customer (and also the doctor's son), he once let me ride his prized bicycle.

The most skilled service professionals in town were the mechanic, blacksmith, pharmacist, and doctor. I observed the mechanic closely during my regular visits to Hadad's flour mill, located just north of Banfi Castle. The mill's main mechanic was a huge man with tools swinging in his hands or hanging from his pockets. He maintained the large, wood-fired steam generator that turned the mill wheel and other mill equipment by means of a long leather belt. The mill ground all the locally produced grains into flour and pressed the sunflower seeds into cooking oil. The mill was key to the town's food supply. The mechanic also serviced the electric power generator that ran my father's x-ray machine when it went on the fritz.

The blacksmith made horseshoes, shoed the horses, and performed the town's incidental ironwork. I watched him hammer the iron shoe into shape after heating the iron in a manually fired grill. Then he fit and nailed the smoking shoe to the horse's hoof. Both the blacksmith's and the mechanic's jobs impressed me with the importance of iron to Hadad's well-being. Iron was critical not only for the horses' shoes, but also for the mill's generator, the Banfi's tractor (the only one in town), and Father's x-ray equipment. It also was necessary for the incidental repairs to the farm truck that appeared in town each season to haul fatted pigs to slaughter in some distant city. Even as recently as the early 1940s, the Industrial Revolution still had little impact on life in Hadad.

The town pharmacist was a tall, mustachioed man who lived in a house just behind his pharmacy and opposite the synagogue in the town center. His pharmacy practice survived mostly by filling prescriptions written by my father. Rows of bottles bearing mysterious drugs and potions lined the pharmacy shelves. Swimming in one large bottle of clear liquid were leeches, thought to cure certain illnesses by sucking bad blood from a patient's body. I frequently walked up the few steps from the street into the pharmacy to visit the pharmacist. He gave me the promotional toys distributed by drug companies like Bayer. The pharmacist also had a flock of pigeons that flew out of the coop in his backyard, circled the market square in a flock, and swooped back into their individual roosts.

Besides the cobbler and the tailor, the other prominent Jewish men in Hadad included the Orthodox rabbi, Hebrew teacher, synagogue caretaker, two store owners, a tavern owner (our last landlord), and of course, my father. They all pursued non-farming occupations, and were hard working and self-reliant. The Hebrew teacher, who taught both Gabriel and me, had other jobs as well: he slaughtered animals to ensure they were kosher and also helped look after the synagogue.

The Orthodox Jewish men stood out from others in Hadad because of their black tailored pants, jackets, vests, and hat, or *keppele*, that they wore all day. They ate only kosher food and washed their hands several times a day, before meals and prayers. Many Jewish boys wore long white shirts under their jackets from which white strings, or *tsitsas*, hung down to their thighs. They used the tsitsas for prayer and for turning the pages of religious texts so as not to touch the paper with their fingers. Our family, by contrast, wore only Western-style clothing. My father dressed in a suit with a necktie, just like the mayor, teachers, priest, and pharmacist, none of whom were Jewish. Clothing styles reflected one's position in the community.

The Jewish families in Hadad shared a public bath, or *mikva*. The mikva was essentially a large square hole, about five feet square and five feet deep, dug in the middle of a room inside a small house and lined with supporting beams. To enter the mikva, you walked down about six steps before reaching the bottom. The mikva was deep enough for me to stand in water up to my shoulders and wide enough to accommodate three or four people at a time. The water was heated in pots on a nearby stove and dumped into the bath as required. Men and women bathed separately, and usually did so on Fridays before going to the synagogue. The mikva attracted no special attention, despite its religious exclusivity, because the house looked just like every other house in town. I never saw or overheard my parents talk about using the mikva. I preferred my own small wooden tub at home, with Mother pouring warm water over my head from a pitcher while I scrubbed with soap.

As a Jewish boy approaching age thirteen, I had to learn to read Hebrew so that I could recite in front of the congregation at my bar mitzvah and show that I had come of age as a responsible adult. I studied with the Hebrew teacher and spent considerable time in synagogue reading Hebrew from a textbook. This put me in the company of highly religious Jewish boys, who appeared to understand what they were reading. I never did. Instead, I became quickly bored and flew out the synagogue door as soon as the lesson ended. I usually headed off to the grocery store next to our home on the main street. Joska Richter's mother owned the grocery store and always had chocolates and cookies waiting for me. Without ever understanding the Hebrew text to be recited, I eventually memorized it. Thus prepared, I satisfactorily acquitted myself from the synagogue pulpit, standing nervously before the whole congregation, including my parents and brother.

Growing up in Hadad, I never felt any discrimination because of my religion. I was equally welcome in the homes of Jews and non-Jews alike and related easily with everyone in town, regardless of his or her religion. At Christmas I sang in the Protestant church choir with my Christian friends, and at Easter I visited their homes to hunt for the carefully painted

Easter eggs after spraying everyone with perfume (a local tradition). Also, as a senior Boy Scout in Hadad, I recited nationalistic prayers and gave speeches before large crowds of townspeople who gathered on holidays in front of the World War I memorial. My prominent participation in such local civic ceremonies made me feel like a well-accepted member of the community.

From ages five through eleven (1934–1940), I attended kindergarten and elementary school in Hadad. Because my parents were not particularly religious, they sent me to public rather than parochial school. All the other local Jewish children attended the *heider*, a school in the synagogue, or they studied at home. The kindergarten was right next to the elementary school in Hadad; both were located down a side street across from the post office. The elementary school was small, with multiple grades per classroom. One small schoolroom also served as the Roman Catholic chapel, attended mostly by Romanians, who had no separate church in town. Another distinct feature of the elementary school was its location near a honey-producing beehive situated on a hill above the schoolyard and close to the Reformed Church. My fascination with bees drew me regularly to their hive. I watched as the honey was removed and stored, and for my interest I was rewarded with periodic bee stings.

After finishing elementary school in Hadad, I attended two other middle schools (gymnasiums) from ages eleven to fourteen (fall 1940–spring 1944)—one in Kolozsvar and another in Szamosujvar. I attended private school in Kolozsvar for less than a year, while living in a rented apartment with my mother. Mother worked there as an assistant to a well-known female dermatologist in private practice. We often visited Mother's stepmother, her sister Magda Israel, and her half-brother Ervin, who lived together in an apartment there. On weekends, Mother and I strolled through Kolozsvar's parks, visiting the lake and the English garden to watch the swans and resting on benches to admire the church's beautiful façade and the adjacent statue of King Mathias on horseback.

Following my brief schooling in Kolozsvar, I transferred to gymnasium in Szamosujvar. Initially I stayed with my Frenkel grandparents, who lived within walking distance of the school. After about six months, however, my father bought a house on the very same block where my grandparents lived. I moved into that house with Aunt Magda and Uncle Ervin to finish my schooling in Szamosujvar. Aunt Magda took excellent care of Ervin and me, serving us all kinds of good food that we could not get at Grandmother Frenkel's home because of her religious dietary restrictions.

Like Kolozsvar, although smaller in size, Szamosujvar was also a city that had its own train station. Standing on a bridge over the tracks, I frequently watched trains passing through the station. The Szamos River flowed not far from the city center, and provided enough fish to support commercial fishermen who hauled in their catch using nets. Near the river was the beautiful central park, with a small lake where I went swimming in summer and skating in winter.

The Szamosujvar gymnasium was formal, progressive, and academically excellent. I studied literature, mathematics, Latin, and German, and sang in the school choir. The choir performed in the local Armenian church near Grandmother's store; the church was renowned for a painting attributed to Rembrandt or one of his students. The gymnasium had an athletic facility, with ropes for climbing, horses for gymnastics, and a basketball court. Every day, the students assembled in the schoolyard to perform calisthenics. In one class we were asked to identify where we were born. When my turn came, I stood up and reported mischievously that I was born in bed. For this remark, the teacher pulled my ear and expelled me for the day. My uncle Feri Frenkel (Cili and Morton's son) had attended this same school and apparently was also a prankster. One day I discovered that he had left his name etched on a school windowsill.

To celebrate Hungarian national holidays, the school authorities assembled the student body in front of the school. There we sang the Hungarian national anthem and watched a military parade. Soldiers dressed in their ornate national costumes and police wearing their distinctive hats crowned with cock feathers marched before the student body. Nationalistic fervor was running high at the time and was strongly aligned with Germany.

During those four years attending school away from Hadad, I eagerly awaited every holiday and summer vacation. I missed my many friends, both young and old. I missed the fields and the farms. I missed the town's many activities—religious, civic, and social. I missed my regular meals at home and my warm welcomes at friends' houses. Growing up in Hadad, my life was idyllic. I felt embraced and loved. I never had a fight with anyone and never even had a serious argument. Peaceful Hadad was my home, my shelter, my happiness. Sadly, this tranquility abruptly ended in April 1944, when Father summoned me home from school in Szamosujvar. German and Hungarian Nazis had taken control of Hungary and had started causing problems for Jews.

PART II: THE TERROR

ABANDON EVERY HOPE, ALL YOU WHO ENTER.
I saw these words spelled out in somber colors
inscribed along the ledge above a gate;
"Master," I said, "these words I see are cruel."

Dante Alighieri, *Inferno*

4.
Driven from Home

In April 1944, shortly after returning to Hadad, I had a startling experience. Around noon one day, as I walked down the main street toward home, an open passenger car painted military green, like a jeep, drove past me carrying three German soldiers dressed in field uniforms. Since motor vehicles were rare in Hadad and I had never laid eyes on a German soldier, the appearance of the Germans and their military vehicle so close to home gave me a sudden fright. At the time, however, I had no idea of its terrible import. To this very day, I get chills just recalling it! The vehicle stopped momentarily for one of those soldiers to address a peasant.

I stopped walking, turned around, and went up to the jeep to hear what was being said. "How do we get to Aichelin's house?" the soldier asked. After getting directions, they headed off the main street past the high concrete wall of Degenfeld Castle toward the lower part of town where the Aichelins lived. Immediately I hurried past the Richters' grocery store toward home, only one house away, to tell my mother what I had just seen and heard. She suspected that the German soldiers were calling upon the Lutheran minister, Reverend Aichelin, who was of German descent, to convey information of potential significance to the Jews living in Hadad. Since the war was remote from Hadad, what could have brought the soldiers here except for something related to Hitler's anti-Semitism?

Welcoming German soldiers to their home seemed strange behavior for the Aichelins, although they were the most prominent Germans in Hadad. We waited anxiously to learn why the soldiers had visited them. Our anxiety increased when rumors began circulating around town that all the Jews would be deported. My mother decided to investigate. The Aichelins were family friends—their two daughters had grown up with Gabriel and me, and Mrs. Aichelin and my mother were close. So Mother visited Mrs. Aichelin to learn what the soldiers had said and how it might affect us and the other Jews in Hadad. Calling on their friendship, my mother begged Mrs. Aichelin for information, but initially she refused to say anything. She told Mother the information was "a secret." Only reluctantly, after several days of hesitation, did Mrs. Aichelin finally tell my mother what ultimately turned out to be a lie—that all the Hadad Jews would soon be sent to work in German factories.

We had barely adjusted to this shocking news when the town crier appeared on his regular corner in the market square to address the subject. He announced publicly that every person of Jewish faith must wear a yellow star of a certain size on the upper left side of his or her outer garment and must not appear on the street during certain hours each day. Furthermore, Jewish children could no longer attend public school, a decree that affected only me since all the other Jewish children in town attended parochial school. Overnight, peaceful Hadad had become a very scary place. Our Hungarian neighbors, like the Richters, said nothing to us about what was happening. Either they knew nothing or, like us, they were too afraid to discuss this startling turn of events.

As a result of this anti-Jewish edict, I no longer could venture from the house without asking my father's permission. And this he routinely denied. I could not go out to play with my friends. I could not even visit Joska, who lived right next door. Until this edict, I had climbed over the low wooden fence between our two homes several times a day to play with Joska. Now that was out of the question. Furthermore, simple routines like shopping in town with Mother became embarrassing since we had to wear the yellow star. Strange foreboding hovered in the air.

Next came the public reading of further restrictive decrees. Then, local zealots surfaced to enforce them. I was surprised to see our Hungarian barber among the most active of these zealots—the friendly barber who regularly cut my hair and once let me ride his bicycle. Every day the police summoned Jewish men to the police station one by one for interrogation about their assets, including any hidden jewelry or money. To extract information, the interrogators even beat up some of the men. These newly aggressive Hadad residents had seized the opportunity to rob their Jewish neighbors. Local police issued orders similar to the one reproduced below.

Without exception, Hadad's non-Jewish citizens remained silent within their homes, as if these strange happenings to their Jewish neighbors were none of their business. Perhaps they too were just scared. I had no way of

ORDER

I have taken command of this "Ghetto."

The police will carry out my orders. The use of their guns will be in accordance with regulations. I will punish every deviation from the rules. I demand the literal observation of regulations. I am calling upon every Jew, that:

1. Those valuables (money, jewelry, gold, silver, platinum, paper assets) that are in anyone's possession, are to be delivered to the acquisition team today between 16-20 hours.

2. Anyone who, for whatever reason, gave a valuable to a Christian after March 22 is to report such action in writing today between 16-20 hours to the same team. The listing has to be in detail; what objects, of what value, to whom (exact name, occupation, town, street and number) when and for what reason were the objects handed over. Under the signature of the person filing the report list the occupation and the declared residence address. The report is to be signed by two witnesses. Those who know of such events have equal obligations of reporting them.

3. The family that possesses food in excess of what it requires for 14 days is to deliver such excess food today between 16-20 hours to the same team.

Starting tomorrow assisted by the Ghetto police I will search for those who have not obeyed the above order and will send same to a punishment camp. This order is to be posted in every doorway, and on every floor on multi-level buildings.

Nagyvarad, 1944 May 10
The Police Commander and the Ghetto Governor

knowing, however, because we no longer had contact with anyone. The sole exception was the Gypsy woman who had been our family's maid. One day she appeared on the main road in front of our house, crying inconsolably. I could see the pain in her eyes, which left me with a sense of dread. Only fourteen years old at the time, I was amazed at this simple woman's public display of such powerful emotions. In fact, she was the only one in our town who seemed empathetic toward us. Her spontaneous outpouring of grief sounded like a warning of something unimaginable.

The sick and the well, the old and the young, even small children, were singled out in these orders for no apparent reason other than being Jewish. Unlike my Christian friends, I was forced to see myself as guilty of something undefined, and I became resentful. Why was I suddenly so different from other people in Hadad, and why was I isolated from my longtime friends? What had I done to deserve such ostracism? I no longer could visit Joska next door or call upon Uncle Mihaly or Moses Adorjan at the Banfi farm. Mostly, I sat on our front porch peering out into the street just to observe what was happening

Sick people continued to call upon my father for treatment by walking up the path to our kitchen. But fear was written all over their faces. Overnight, our closeness to these familiar patients vanished. Because Father was the medical doctor for the whole community, we hoped and trusted that at least we would be spared whatever treatment was in store for the other Jews. While Father continued his medical practice, Mother, Gabriel, and I mostly remained indoors, nervous and out of sight.

Listening to the radio now more intently, we knew that the war front was approaching us. The Russian army was slowly driving the retreating German and Hungarian armies in our direction. Romania, Hungary (including Hadad), and Austria stood astride the Russian route to Germany. In this tense atmosphere, our parents secretly arranged to turn over all of our valuables, like gold rings and silverware, to Count and Countess Banfi for safekeeping with their own possessions. Sensing that Communist Russia was unlikely to respect his royal status, the count decided to hide his personal assets from possible confiscation and graciously offered to help us. We took to the Banfis our family's small cache of now long-lost valuables, which the Banfis planned to secrete somewhere out of town along with their own considerable wealth. Curiously, the Banfis and we were both at risk, albeit for different reasons—they from the Communists and we from the Nazis. In Hadad, at this point, the only secure people were the fascist Hungarians, who were few but surprisingly militant, and the more numerous German/Swabians, who included the Reverend Aichelin and his family.

In early May 1944, about ten days after the German soldiers appeared in Hadad, the town crier announced that the next day at a given hour all Jews must present themselves in the market square, carrying personal possessions in no more than two suitcases per person. At the appointed hour that next day, we were packed and ready to join the other Jews in the square when a Hungarian policeman knocked on our door. He walked into our kitchen to announce that, for the present, our family was excluded from deportation. We should remain in our home. As soon as he left our house, the town square began to fill with the Jewish families. Since the square was near our house, I tried to observe this gathering from our porch, but the adjacent building blocked my view. Unable to see what was going on, I still could hear the commotion and wailing that came from the square.

While I sat on the porch, the noise gradually increased as the town's Jewish population started walking down the main street not twenty yards away from me. The rabbi in his religious garb, the tailor, the shoemaker, the elderly weighted down with handbags, and the mothers clutching crying infants—all struggled to move forward with all the possessions they could carry in their two allotted suitcases. A few Hungarian policemen, wearing black hats sprouting cock feathers, guarded this mass of humanity and shouted at them repeatedly to stay in line. Babies cried; old people moaned. The scene was all pain and confusion. Standing in our home by the window, we watched helplessly as this pitiable procession passed by on the road below us. We seemed invisible to these distracted deportees, who made no eye contact with us.

Watching this scene, I became consumed by fear. Evil had descended from nowhere upon peaceful Hadad. Without explanation, it had taken control of these countless innocent lives, with no regard for their age or health, just because they were Jews. Our street eventually emptied of people. This left a strange and troubling silence in our home. The police were marching the entire Jewish population, bags in hand, young and old alike, the seven miles to Szilagy Cseh, presumably to the train station. My family now felt that we were marked people—the arbitrary treatment and yellow stars were visible proof of that. But we had no idea whether or when the authorities would target us. All we could do was wait anxiously inside our small apartment and hope that Father's reputation would protect us.

Our wait was short. Approximately one week after the deportation of Hadad's Jews, a policeman appeared at our door. He informed us that we must begin to pack no more than two small suitcases per person and prepare to leave the next day for the distant Transylvanian town of Mikoujfalu (Micfalau), near the southeastern border with Romania (see Map 2). Father was reassigned there as a doctor. News that our relocation was within Hungary and that Father could continue his medical practice sparked a glimmer of hope. Perhaps we would wind up living and working at peace in this new town, with Gabriel and me reenrolling in school, Mother managing a new household, and Father rebuilding his practice.

Father left Hadad ahead of us by horse carriage, using his regular driver, the same man he had relied upon for many years when visiting bedridden patients in neighboring towns. Mother, Gabriel, and I followed two days later. Because our travel bags were small, we left most of our meaningful possessions inside the home, including Father's x-ray machine and the other contents of his medical office. Our resident Jewish landlord was gone, so no one was left behind to look out for our home and property. All the non-Jews were avoiding us. As we left home, we locked our front door as usual. Thus far we had been lucky, and we remained naïvely hopeful that no harm would befall us. So, displaying yellow stars on our outer coats, my mother, my brother, and I departed Hadad, never imagining that we were now destitute, with little chance of returning to Hadad alive.

Father's driver took us by horse carriage to the Szilagy Cseh train station without any police escort. At that time, we did not know that the Szilagy Cseh rail stop had served as the transfer point for shipping the Hadad Jews to a temporary ghetto in Szatmar, further north, near the Transylvania border. The semblance of normalcy to our departure by train belied our circumstances. After reaching the train station in the early morning darkness, I began to feel afraid as we sat there by ourselves in an empty passenger railcar, waiting for the train to pull out. I had departed from this same station many times to visit my grandparents in Szamosujvar and Kolozsvar, but that morning I was frightened because we were headed under strange circumstances to an unfamiliar destination.

The uneventful, ten-hour train ride from Szilagy Cseh southeast to Mikoujfalu in Hungarian Transylvania took us through forests and fields that looked much like those around Hadad. We spent the ride uneasily absorbed in our own thoughts, not knowing what to expect. We had no inkling that this would be our family's last civilized train ride together. We arrived that evening in Mikoujfalu, a border town with Romania at the edge of the Carpathian Mountains. The town's rolling hills, groves of pine trees, and vast meadows engendered momentary feelings of tranquility and thoughts of safety. Traveling unguarded, we trusted that everything would work out. We were still uninformed about what was happening to the Jews. Had we been more aware or even suspicious of the government's evil motives for relocating us, we could have taken advantage of the lack of police surveillance to make a dash for freedom. The Romanian border was barely five miles away from Mikoujfalu, and the Romanian city of Brasov was only twenty-five miles away.

From the train station we walked into Mikoujfalu against the backdrop of snowcapped Carpathians. The houses near the center of Mikoujfalu were densely packed, but toward the fringes of town and into the nearby valley and distant hills, they gradually spread out and became sparse. Mother, Gabriel, and I moved into an apartment in a house that Father had found for us. We shared the house with its owners, a non-Jewish family, and Mother used the owners' kitchen to cook our food. Father had located his medical office in a separate house on the same street and planned to resume his medical practice there.

Herds of sheep and numerous other animals wandered about the valleys surrounding Mikoujfalu. Despite this rural setting, however, Mikoujfalu seemed more connected to the outside world than Hadad. From our new home, we could see trains passing regularly through the station, sometimes stopping to offload and pick up passengers. Mikoujfalu had a well-known spa, located near the train station, that attracted out-of-towners to this primitive resort town. We saw no German or Hungarian soldiers there or any other signs of military activity.

Our parents tried to imbue life in Mikoujfalu with a sense of normalcy. Father saw patients in his outside office. Mother cooked, cleaned, and brought order to our little two-room apartment. I carried earthen jugs to fetch carbonated water from a nearby well that provided our drinking water. The local farmers used the same carbonated well water to irrigate the nearby fields. Neither Gabriel nor I enrolled in school. Instead, I passed my days exploring the meadow near our house, and Gabriel buried himself in a book. I made no friends or even casual acquaintances in Mikoujfalu. There were no Jews in town, but it never occurred to us that they might already have been deported like the Jews in Hadad. Knowing no one and unsure about what might happen to us next, I remained anxious. Though pastoral and pleasant, our new town was exile.

After about two weeks, just as we'd started to settle into life at Mikoujfalu, we once again received unexpected orders to pack—this time, only one suitcase each—and to present ourselves at the station the next day to take a train. This time the authorities made no mention of Father's practice or our destination. These troubling omissions together with the further luggage limitation gripped us all with a terrible uncertainty. Had they changed their minds about the value of having a medical doctor in Mikoujfalu? Was my father's professional expertise no longer needed in Transylvania?

The next day, May 22, 1944, we found ourselves the only passengers at the station—and, more disturbingly, we were suddenly under arrest. In a state of shock, we boarded the train in the custody of a policeman. The policeman rode with us in stony silence, wearing the familiar black hat crowned with cock feathers. This train ride was shorter, only one or two hours, at which point we arrived at the small city of Segesvar (Sighisoara). Upon our arrival, some civilians took custody of us from the policeman and walked us a short distance into the grassy courtyard of a brick factory. There we were greeted with an astonishing sight.

The courtyard was jammed with people covering every bit of available space both inside and outside the factory building. Apparently the authorities had transported all the Jews from the surrounding towns into this dismal place. It was sheer pandemonium. Some people cooked meals by small wood fires out in the open, others washed clothes or cut hair, and screaming children ran everywhere. People slogged through the mud that covered the entire courtyard, everyone in everyone else's way. Abruptly and unceremoniously, we were corralled with the dispossessed in this bedlam, and we became terrified.

Hungarian Nazis acting as camp guards harshly summoned people, mostly men, into a small house to be interrogated. Even from far away in the courtyard, we could hear the screams coming from inside the house as the interrogators beat these men. The interrogators were trying to coerce them into divulging where they had hidden money and jewelry left behind in their homes. Several men came out bleeding, crying in pain, and moaning about the beating they had just received. Hungarian thugs selected these particular men for interrogation based upon information about their valuables gathered from their neighbors. Coming from tranquil Hadad, I found this brutal scene horrifying. Furthermore, we were trapped in this hellish madhouse. The only quiet came at evening when we slept in our clothes under a shed in the courtyard.

About a week after we arrived at the brick factory, our names appeared on a long list posted on the side of the shed. Accompanying the list of names were orders to pack a small bag and to line up at a certain hour the next morning on the highway in front of the gate. The orders said nothing about where we were going. How very sinister it all seemed—the way we were transported in stages, moved from place to place, limited each time as to the amount of permissible baggage, and uninformed about our destination. We little realized at the time that a dark master plan underlay these seemingly arbitrary logistics. The following day, we obediently left the brick factory, as ordered, each of us carrying only one small luggage bag. It was far lighter than the luggage with which we left Hadad less than a month earlier. We remained wholly ignorant of our destination, perhaps some German factory—or so we still assumed.

5.
Herded To Hell

The group leaving the factory that day consisted of five hundred to a thousand people. After we assembled on the highway, the Hungarian fascists and police directed us to line up five abreast and then march to the railroad station about a mile away. The resulting queue stretched the entire distance from the brickyard to the station. As we neared the train platform, I saw cattle cars for the first time, with their open doors facing the yard. German SS soldiers stood around the platform in their gray uniforms with their menacing dogs on leashes, and one soldier sat atop each railcar with a rifle in his lap. Obviously the Germans were ready and waiting for the Hungarians to hand us over to them. The soldiers distributed us exactly seventy people to each car, and then divided the car into two groups, with thirty-five on either side of an open passage that stretched across the middle of the car between the two side doors. In this central passage the soldiers placed a chamber pot and a water bucket with a cup.

Outside the train and standing on the platform, guards screamed orders to each other and to us. German officers dressed in their distinct tight-fitting SS uniforms and wearing black boots controlled everything. Inside our car, Gabriel quickly secured us a corner below a small barred window. One woman pleaded to leave the train to go to the bathroom, and the guard replied summarily, *"Scheissen sie in ihrem rock!"* ("Shit in your dress!") From here on, we were transported under tight security by German guards holding loaded guns. On this train, we were no longer traveling as passengers but as freight.

So began our deportation from Hungary in late May 1944, driven off like so much cattle. We still expected that our destination was some German factory, where we would labor in the war effort. Jammed into the hot cattle car, I sat with my small suitcase on the bare floor together with my parents, Gabriel, and sixty-six strangers. As soon as the train started moving, I began to panic. It quickly became apparent that I had lost my freedom. I had no idea what lay ahead. Next to me on the floor by the window sat a very fat woman whose offensive body odor we had to endure throughout the entire trip. She perspired in the heat and smelled terrible, but there was no escaping her. Almost no conversation took place within the car. I saw my bewildered mother and nervous father sitting uncomfortably on the car floor, staring awkwardly at one another, their faces fixed with fright. They could offer Gabriel and me no comfort.

The train proceeded very slowly, and the ride lasted a long five to six days (see Map 4). From the brick factory, we traveled through the lush Transylvanian countryside and across the Hungarian border into Czechoslovakia. Each day during the trip we received a piece of bread and margarine, hot coffee made with chicory, and watery soup. A German soldier opened the car door just enough to push in two buckets containing the daily ration of food and water. This procedure left the prisoners to distribute everything equally. One person usually assumed responsibility for handing out the food. Given the small quantity of food, however, fights often erupted as people rushed to the center of the car, anxious to get their meager share.

Every day I stared at the passing green countryside through the iron grill on the small car window and thought about Hadad, my sweet hometown, lying somewhere not too far over the horizon. Recalling my happy and carefree days roaming those Hadad fields actually sustained me during the long and uncomfortable journey. Surely if I could be imprisoned so suddenly and unreasonably, I could be freed just as abruptly and unexpectedly—or so I hoped. For the time being, however, I was trapped in this locked cattle car guarded by armed German SS. Why was I here? That troubling question kept nagging at me, but I knew that my parents could provide no answer. I pondered, *Are Jews any different from non-Jews, and are the German guards not human beings like the rest of us?* Whenever one of the SS came close to me, I looked carefully at his face for some sign of compassion for us. I never saw any.

After crossing the border from Hungary into Czechoslovakia, the train soon entered Poland. I could see many large factories with tall smoking chimneys. Their sheer size was unlike anything that I had seen in the agricultural towns and cities of Transylvania. The huge structures were intimidating, as were the extensive railroad yards where our hissing steam locomotive stopped to refuel and take on water. The yards contained numerous tracks, freight trains, and terminal buildings with unpronounceable Polish names. The immensity of the scene was overwhelming. Everything became even more frightening when the SS began shouting during their changing of the guard at our various station stops.

Until our train actually entered Poland, most of us thought we were headed for a work detail in Germany. After a few days on the train, however, it became clear that Mrs. Aichelin's report and the circulating rumors about our German destination were false. Had the three German soldiers who visited her in Hadad lied about Germany's plans for us, or had she lied to us about their plans? For my father, this apparent deception was especially troubling. He was the respected medical doctor for Hadad and its environs and a veteran of the Austro-Hungarian Army in World War I. With his medical credentials and war record, Father could not believe that his family would come to any harm, despite our dire circumstances. We all clung desperately to that faint hope. After all, Mrs. Aichelin reported that the secret German plan was to make us factory workers. In any event, we still remained together as a family. Because of this fact, we never considered fleeing.

As we wended our way northward, the cities of Poland passed by our train window. Looking through the grating on the small car window, Gabriel saw a long freight train typical of those usually carrying gravel. But this train was loaded to the brim with baggage—bundles tied together, children's backpacks, and elegant pigskin suitcases with labels from international hotels. At one stop, while peering through the window grill, I saw some Polish railroad workers, one of whom raised his chin and drew his finger across his throat, signifying that we would all be executed.

I immediately turned to Gabriel and said, "Did you see that gesture? We are going to be killed!"

He answered, "Yes, but don't tell our parents."

During the same stop, the guards opened the train door to allow my mother to go to the toilet. Gabriel and I went along with her to hold up a bed sheet in order to hide her from public view as she relieved herself.

Finally, on June 3, 1944, the train pulled into a Polish station with a sign that read *Oswicziem*. The Germans called it *Auschwitz*. As the locomotive took on water, we overheard the guards' conversation indicating that we were near our final destination. At this stop, the train slowly reversed direction. The locomotive, now in the rear, began pushing instead of pulling and diverted the train onto a spur track. The spur led into a vast flat complex made up of single-story wooden barracks stretching as far as the eye could see. Around each of the barracks was a small yard surrounded by an electrified barbed-wire fence supported by intermittent posts with lights on top of each post. At every fence corner was a wooden guard tower manned by a soldier with a gun. As the train halted, I saw that we had arrived inside a camp, surrounded on all sides by a barbed-wire fence. This was the destination that no one was willing to disclose to us—not the Germans, not the Hungarians, not even our friends the Aichelins, assuming they knew the truth.

Outside the train, I heard German spoken. Then the door on one side of our train opened abruptly and men began yelling, *"Raus! Raus! Raus!"* (*"Out! Out! Out!"*) Several of these men climbed into our train and began pushing us out. This all happened so quickly that we were stunned. These men were prisoners, dressed in striped clothes. They looked grim and deadened—lifeless machines, disembodied voices transmitting orders. I assumed that some unimaginable experience must have befallen them to cause their strange, inhuman state. A small square was cut out at the back of their jackets and the sides of their pant legs, and they wore a number on the front of their jackets above the heart. They were marked and numbered, possibly to prevent their escape. Conversation with them was impossible. They grimly hissed, "You all will die here." Strangely, their words did not frighten me, as they should have, because nothing that was happening seemed real.

I climbed down from the train amid the flow of people, trying to hold onto my parents' hands. Just as we stepped off the train, these same men herded us into a column, standing five abreast. People were tripping over one another—mothers holding children or walking beside them holding their hands, men carrying bags and packages containing their sole remaining possessions. We had barely anything left of the small amount of luggage with which we started our trip. We held our coats,

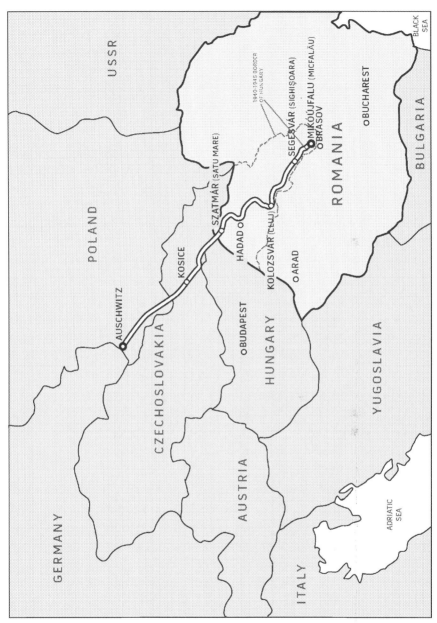

Map 4: This map depicts the approximate route of the five- to six-day train ride that the Frenkel family was forced to take by cattle car from Mikoujfalu (Micfalau) in eastern Transylvania, then part of Hungary, to Auschwitz Concentration Camp in Poland, where they arrived on June 3, 1944.

and I also clutched my leather-covered Bayer pocket diary, which I liked because of its smell. I intended to keep at least this small personal item as long as possible. Standing in line, I noticed a strange-smelling smoke in the air, which I learned a few days later came from cremation of dead bodies. I assumed the dead were people who had become ill and died here. Only after my camp experience did I learn that these were the bodies of murdered Jews.

After disembarking the train, the large mass of people inched forward toward several German soldiers wearing black boots and standing mid-road, blocking our way. We became separated from Mother because they directed women to the right and men to the left. I expected that she would eventually rejoin us and never suspected that this was the last time I would ever see her.

The central figure standing before this throng was a tall man wearing a white doctor's coat, SS cap, and black boots. He was the notorious Dr. Josef Mengele, I later learned, the perpetrator of sadistic experiments on live human beings. Father's reaction on seeing him typified his positive outlook. "Great! A doctor! I will speak to him. But first, I will take off my hat, so that he sees my white hair and treats me with more respect." After approaching and speaking to Mengele, Father reported to Gabriel, "I told him that there were doctors on this transport, and I offered our services in a professional capacity." He said that Mengele replied, "Fine, Herr colleague. Would you all stand aside." And so we did.

After the line of people from the train thinned out, Mengele signaled to our group containing all the doctors, including Gabriel and me, that we should proceed off to the left along with one other group already headed in that direction. Later we learned that our group was destined for hard labor. Unbeknownst to us at the time, this was a lucky turn of fate. Passing to the right of soldiers facing us, we trudged down a narrow alley enclosed by barbed wire toward an open iron gate. A metal sign reading *"Arbeit Macht Frei"* (*"Work Makes You Free"*) overarched the gate. (See photograph.)

Tired, ragged, and frightened, we dragged ourselves into a flat, treeless courtyard near one or two wooden barracks and within a barbed-wire perimeter. Standing and looking about the maze of barracks that stretched far into the distance, I tried to comprehend my surroundings. It seemed unbelievable that anyone would visit this upon us. We had done nothing to harm these people or to deserve such mistreatment. Before long, the "capos" appeared before us. Prisoners themselves, these capos began shouting for us to undress and proceed toward some four or five grim-faced barbers off in the distance. Upon reaching the barber, we were ordered to sit down for the mandatory haircut. The barbers cut everyone's hair right down to the scalp, leaving only a narrow swath of hair that stretched from the forehead to the base of the skull.

As we stood about the yard, shorn and naked, the capos ordered that we leave our clothes on the ground and proceed toward a shed that housed showers. I carefully stuffed my leather diary under my shirt and left it on the ground where I could find it easily after returning from the shower. Pushed forward in groups of about twenty, we stumbled into a small room with a cement floor and a drain. Water poured from metal sprinklers placed high on the walls, getting us wet. Initially I felt embarrassed at standing naked for the first time in my life before so many strangers, but soon I focused on enjoying the hot shower. It was very brief, however, because the capos soon ordered us out of the shower room. As we left the room, the capos threw over the top of our whole group two large white bed sheets, intended for common use as drying towels.

Even before we had completely dried ourselves, the capos hurried us into an empty barrack located adjacent to the shower room and ordered us to line up five abreast. Standing before our large group of naked men, a German officer made a speech about how we must work in the camp. Then, in threatening tones, he screamed that we must give up any valuables hidden inside our bodies. This order sounded bizarre to me. Why would anyone concern himself with treasure when his very life was at stake? Furthermore, I could not imagine anyone hiding gold, silver, or diamonds inside some body cavity. In any event, no one stepped forward. Either they had nothing to hand over or were determined to keep it. Fortunately, neither the capos nor the SS followed up, as we had expected, to search our bodies.

In what turned out to be a typical camp practice, capos stood immediately beside the German officer who addressed us, ready to carry out his orders. After the officer's speech, we exited the barrack in single file, and the capos handed us our new uniforms—striped pants and a matching jacket of thin cotton material. Because our route from the showers did not proceed back through the courtyard from which we entered, I could not search for, and never did find, my precious leather diary.

The capos were Gypsies, Jews, or other internees who sold themselves to the Germans as camp wardens simply to survive. These SS minions ordered us around, tormented us, beat us, and generally instilled fear throughout our stay at Auschwitz. At any time and for no apparent reason, a capo might single someone out for physical punishment. They randomly hit people with wooden sticks, especially one man whom they regularly beat simply because he had a long nose. They chased after him around the yard with sticks, beating him all the while until he fell down. I was never beaten or struck while there, but the daily unprovoked beatings of others unnerved me and kept everyone constantly on edge. Reading their body language, I started to understand how the guards and capos behaved. Scared and cautious, I stayed out of their way.

Among our group were the fifteen to twenty doctors Mengele had initially segregated from other passengers on the transport. These doctors stood about one day, my father among them. Each one described how skilled he was in his particular medical specialty and how much the Germans needed his skills. One especially tall and distinguished doctor stood out in the group. He asserted that his specialty had unique value to the Germans and that, if called upon by them, he would readily offer his services. Since Father participated in this professional discussion, I deduced that we all were destined for some special assignment in the German war effort. Yet no officers, guards, or capos ever told us why we were sent to the camp, what purpose the camp served, or why we were under armed guard. Indeed, apart from this one discussion among the doctors, the camp internees spoke very little among themselves. Life itself seemed to hang suspended.

Inside the barracks, wooden bunks were stacked five high and lined the entire floor from one end to the other. Down the middle of the barracks, extending its entire length, was an open drainage ditch. While my father and brother slept with the other inmates on the wooden bunks, I stretched out alone on the dirt floor directly over the empty drainage ditch, just to get away from the mass of people crowded into the multiple tiers of bunks. I slept with my feet on one side of the ditch, my upper body on the other, and my bottom suspended over it.

One day a German guard handed each of us a plain postcard to send home to someone. This looked very suspicious, and we decided it was an SS trick designed to make us reveal the whereabouts of relatives still living in Hungary. Using the addresses on the postcards, the Germans would track down and arrest those Jews who had avoided the roundup and deportation to Auschwitz and remained in hiding. Gabriel and I decided to address our cards to the Reverend Aichelin in Hadad. Perhaps our card would cast some suspicion on him for having betrayed us to the Germans. Throughout my stay inside the Nazi camps, I savored the thought that someday, when the war was over, the Aichelins would be arrested and jailed for collaborating in our unlawful arrest and imprisonment.

Looking through our electrified barbed-wire fence to the adjacent street one day, I saw a group of women in prison uniforms. They were walking toward me behind a cart guarded by armed SS men. As they approached, I searched carefully among them, hoping to see my mother. She was not there. Disappointed and saddened, I became lost in thoughts about her and the warm home, happy childhood, and loving care she gave me.

A neighboring barrack contained prisoners who had spent a long time in the camp. Spontaneously, one of them shouted in my direction, "You will never get out of here alive." I did not know whether to believe him, but I could not imagine that he knew something I had overlooked. Indeed, I assumed that this camp was only an interim phase and eventually we were destined to work in some German factory.

After only two weeks at Auschwitz, the capos told everyone in our section that we were being moved to a transit area where we would board a train. Once in this transit area, we received a more substantial meal than the usual thin soup provided at the camp. The improved fare was reassuring. Watching it being ladled from a barrel onto our metal plates, I relished the prospect of eating something hearty, despite its smelly cheese ingredient. That meal turned out to be our last at Auschwitz. Because our stay at Auschwitz was so short and involved no work assignment, we never received the infamous numerical tattoos on our arms that identified long-term internees.

On June 18, 1944, we left Auschwitz in a group of about a thousand internees, guarded this time by German Luftwaffe (air force) personnel. Their light blue uniforms and more relaxed attitude provided a welcome change from the deadly black uniforms and unremitting seriousness of the dreaded SS. The Luftwaffe guards squeezed us into a waiting train, the usual seventy men per car. Along our route the train pulled into the Dresden station, where I saw civilian passengers walking on the platform. They seemed oblivious to our presence, although we were only a few yards away. In my innocence and trust, I hoped soon to be walking among them on that same platform, a free person.

The train left Dresden and passed through Weimar (see Map 5). The nearness of this cultural center engendered an erudite discussion among some of our group about Goethe and other luminaries of German civilization. The prospect of coming to harm in Goethe's homeland seemed unimaginable to most of us. Such was our denial of reality. Eventually the train stopped and backed through tall trees into the main entrance of Buchenwald, our second concentration camp. Here the guards ordered us to leave the train, again without saying what was in store for us. Thus began our stay at Buchenwald.

6.
Working to Survive

We arrived at Buchenwald on June 18, 1944, and proceeded through an iron gate that was part of the building at the camp's single entrance. (See photograph.) The Buchenwald gate bore a different sign from that at Auschwitz: *"Jedem Das Seine "* (*"To Each His Own"*). On the other side of the gate, as our column turned right through the main courtyard, we each received a prisoner identification number. Presumably this personal number was what the Germans meant by the signage, "to each his own." The prisoner ranks began to stir as everyone examined and compared his new number. Mine was 53999 and Father's 53998. But neither was as easy to remember as Gabriel's number, 54000. I was jealous but unable to exchange numbers with him.

Within a few minutes, which left little time for conversation, the capos ordered everyone to re-form into columns, five abreast, and move forward toward a large gray building with a towering smokestack. Upon reaching the building, the capos directed us, as they had in Auschwitz, to remove our clothes, to leave them on the ground, and to proceed into the shower room before us. There we took a refreshing shower that lasted only minutes. Soon the capos handed each of us a clean pair of pants and a jacket, and tossed some bed sheets at us to dry ourselves. Then they directed us into the lower "Little Camp" about two hundred yards away.

Enclosed by barbed wire and cordoned off from the Main Camp at Buchenwald, the Little Camp contained three or four large tents. Each tent contained numerous rows of wooden bunks stacked high atop one another, as in Auschwitz, and sufficient for two hundred to three hundred prisoners. The Main Camp at Buchenwald seemed more stable and less threatening than the camp at Auschwitz. In conversation, I learned that many Buchenwald prisoners were long-term internees, including some prominent German Communists who had been incarcerated there since 1938.

The veteran internees at the Main Camp were well-informed and talked freely with us about the camp's history. Apparently Buchenwald had been a much scarier place during the four years prior to our arrival. Previously, the camp guards had a practice of hanging captured escapees in front of all the assembled prisoners. Having come this far, I was determined to avoid that fate. Furthermore, I felt that our incarceration could not possibly last another four years, and that I could outlast the camps if I did not succumb to accident or starvation. I resolved then and there to concentrate on my own survival.

Adjacent to the tents in the Little Camp was a wooden shed containing six or seven holes that served as toilets. Outside the barbed-wire perimeter of the tent area and separately enclosed in barbed wire was an assembly yard that stretched up to the camp's main gate. Within this assembly area, the guards counted the prisoners every morning and evening before handing out meals. The morning meal consisted of soup and bread, and the evening meal was simply chicory coffee. Each morning, the guards dispersed the prisoners from the assembly area to various local worksites outside the camp, like the Siemens plant or the Buchenwald stone quarry. We were sent to both sites. On one occasion, I managed to steal away from the work detail at Siemens and hide out for a portion of the day. On my return, Gabriel asked about my whereabouts, and I reported finding and falling asleep in a doghouse.

Standing in line at the assembly area one evening, I overheard a German prisoner next to me hold a short, whispered conversation with an SS officer who had come to take the count. The German prisoner, probably a Communist and a long-term internee, was given charge of us Jews. Holding a personal conversation, rather than barking orders like some crazed animal, was such normal behavior that I thought this SS officer might be human. I naïvely kept looking for signs of hidden compassion in our SS overseers. My youthful optimism persisted throughout the following year in the camps and undoubtedly aided in my survival.

One morning, while awaiting my assignment to a worksite, I saw a group of about a hundred well-dressed and healthy-looking young men pass in formation under the Buchenwald gate, proceed through the main assembly square, and head into a barrack located at the edge of camp. We learned that they were Norwegian students arrested by the Gestapo in Oslo for participating in an anti-Nazi protest. Unlike other Buchenwald prisoners, these students kept their own clothes, received decent rations, enjoyed recreational soccer, and undertook no work details. Just as suddenly as they arrived, they left, repatriated to Norway as free men. Would that we were among them!

Earlier on the day of the students' departure, as we had lined up for the usual head count, I saw an SS officer charge into our group and for no apparent reason viciously beat a man who was obediently standing at attention. Such arbitrary brutality was a daily fact of life in the camps. I examined the facial expressions of this SS officer, trying to deduce his intentions toward me. He looked threatening, so I kept my distance. Despite such pervasive evil surrounding me, I firmly believed it could not last indefinitely and I would survive it.

After a relatively short time at Buchenwald, the authorities transferred our group to our third camp, located in the neighboring city of Zeitz (see Map 5). This camp consisted of tents set up in a grassy area just outside the city proper and next to the Brabag gasoline factory, which extracted oil from coal. A road separated the factory from the camp, which was encircled by a barbed-wire fence. As Nazi camps go, Zeitz was fairly primitive and already showed the effects of Allied bombing.

Our meals at Zeitz arrived twice daily in big pots. We lined up, holding our metal bowls to receive a ladleful of light soup and a small slice of bread. After the morning meal, we walked the hundred feet or so from our camp to the main gate of the factory, where we received our day's work assignment at different jobsites within the factory grounds. The jobs included everything from filling potholes in the street to stacking boxes in the warehouse. I worked primarily in the warehouse of the Swedish company SKF, which supplied Germany with ball bearings.

I unloaded heavy boxes of SKF ball bearings from railcars and stacked them on shelves in the warehouse basement. My goal was to do as little productive work as possible, even creating make-work when I could. When unobserved by the guards, I dropped the boxes on the floor and then restacked them. In addition to Jewish slave laborers, the warehouse workforce also included a few German civilians. Once, a civilian preceded me up the stairs from the basement storeroom. Knowing that I was following immediately behind him and without ever looking back, the

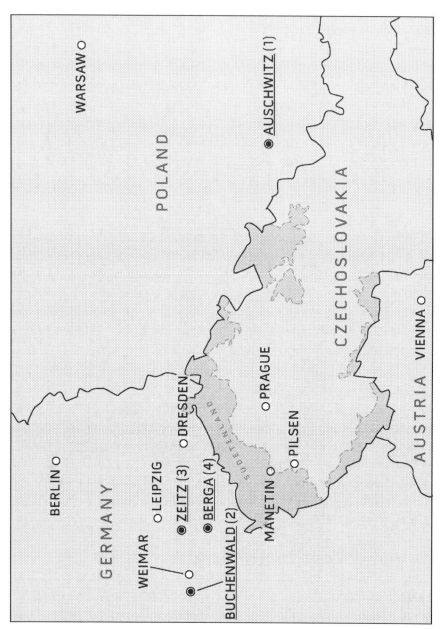

Map 5: This map identifies the location of the four Nazi concentration camps in which I was interred: (1) Auschwitz in southern Poland, and (2) Buchenwald, (3) Zeitz, and (4) Berga in eastern Germany.

civilian set some fruit on the stairs for me. Even ordinary Germans, it seemed, could not afford to have their generosity and compassion for a young prisoner observed by camp guards. On another occasion, however, a female German worker sat down beside me, put her arm around my shoulder, and asked, "Where is your mother?" I was so frightened by this overture from a German that I immediately stood up and walked away without answering her question.

On July 24, 1944, after four weeks at Zeitz, I reached a teenage milestone—age fifteen. Our reduced family, however, had neither the means, opportunity, nor desire to celebrate.

Lifting heavy boxes of ball bearings was plenty strenuous, but it did not compare with unloading railcars. We had to shovel out railroad cars loaded with sand or rocks delivered to Zeitz for use in repairing its roads, badly pockmarked from repeated Allied bombing attacks. Shoveling out this gravel was truly backbreaking work. After emptying the railcars, we spread the gravel over the roadways to level out the potholes and bomb craters. One day a railcar arrived at Zeitz carrying several boxes of food rations instead of the usual construction materials. The car displayed the Red Cross insignia on its door. Unloading the boxes of rations, we momentarily got our hopes up. Alas, the feast was not meant for Jewish internees but for military prisoners. In the minds of the SS, Jews did not qualify as prisoners of war.

As we assembled in the Zeitz camp yard one morning, the air-raid sirens sounded an alarm. Shortly thereafter, a fleet of American bombers flew low overhead, directly above us. They released bombs that exploded on the factory. I was so excited to see the aerial attack that I stood up in the open yard, waving my arms at the pilots, oblivious to the shrapnel flying all around me. Eventually I got hold of myself and hit the ground, or the explosions surely would have killed me. In the aftermath of the attack, I lay there feeling exhilarated like every other prisoner in the camp. Finally, the Allies were coming to our rescue!

Immediately upon hearing the alarm, our German guards scattered, leaving the camp's perimeter momentarily unguarded. Their absence fed my imagination about escaping. Yet it provided no reasonable opportunity for escape. I knew that the German population surrounding the camp would not protect us. Furthermore, if captured, I would be executed like so many other captured escapees. Thoughts of escape were as brief as the bombing run and offered only fleeting relief from our endless labors.

Sitting on my bunk one night at Zeitz, I heard wailing sounds coming from the far end of the tent and decided to investigate. Nearing the sound, I came upon a group of eight to ten very religious Jews, crying to God with tears streaming down their faces, asking what they had done to deserve this punishment. They professed to have observed all the religious rules, accepted all the religious tenets, atoned for all past wrongdoing, and prayed regularly as observant Jews. Over and over again, for a good fifteen to twenty minutes, they sobbed uncontrollably. "What have I done to you, oh Lord, to deserve this punishment? Why have you forsaken me to this torment?" It was a mixture of prayer and lament, Biblical quotes and personal anguish. I found this unselfconscious outpouring of adult grief very upsetting, and I have never forgotten it. The group soon disbanded, everyone returning to his bunk for fear of being identified and punished by guards who might respond to the disturbance.

We labored at Zeitz for about three months. It took a terrible toll on all of us, but especially on Father. The unrelenting labor of lifting, shoveling, and spreading stones for long hours day after day, with little food for sustenance, left us all exceedingly weak and utterly exhausted. My father became very tired and thin. He looked increasingly unfit for this backbreaking daily routine. Although a born optimist, Father had gradually become disillusioned at Zeitz. By the end of our stay there, the guards must have observed his lack of fitness for such hard labor.

About two days after the Allied bomb run, the guards ordered us aboard cattle cars at Zeitz. We soon found ourselves back at Buchenwald. At the next day's assembly, following our return to Buchenwald, the SS guards made us strip and then proceed into a building located in the courtyard of the Little Camp. There, starved and naked, we passed before a group of SS doctors wearing white coats and sitting at a table before us. Intermittently mumbling to one another in disinterested monotones as each of us approached them, these doctors motioned each person either to the left or right. This perfunctory review, we later learned to our horror, constituted a human culling process. Few of us at the time realized the terrible consequence of this seemingly routine procedure. As usual, its true purpose was hidden in order not to alert or panic the unsuspecting victims. Just like so many other life-and-death decisions rendered in the camps, these SS doctors handed down their verdict silently, with a mere gesture.

Unlike all the prior selection processes, this one seemed momentarily reassuring. At least we did not stand around interminably while waiting anxiously for something to happen. In a split second that day, as we appeared before them, one after the other, the SS doctors made their decision. We did not know then that they had just sealed Father's fate. Obviously, in retrospect, they had concluded that Father lacked sufficient strength to undertake the heavy work at our next camp, Berga-Elster. Probably because of our youth, Gabriel and I impressed them differently. So they separated us from Father. With his medical credentials and reputation and his military service in the prior war on the Italian front, Father had steadfastly believed that the Germans would not harm him and his family. How thoroughly deceived he was!

During those last few hours in the Little Camp, we heard rumors that the Germans had imprisoned the former head of the Hungarian government, Admiral Horthy. Rumor had it that he was confined to a military barrack near Buchenwald's infamous stone quarry. We took great satisfaction in Horthy's incarceration, since he had allowed the German deportation of the Transylvanian Jews. (On October 15, 1944, the Nazis did arrest Horthy after his attempt to surrender Hungary to the Russians, and they imprisoned him in Bavaria.)

While we were waiting in the Little Camp at Buchenwald, a Hungarian man approached Gabriel and me with his young son. This man was being separated from his son as the result of the SS selection process, just as Father had been separated from us. The boy's father pleaded with Gabriel and me to look after his son.

As people milled about in our two separate groups before being marched off in different directions, Gabriel and I exchanged final, anxious glances with Father. Of course, no one knew at the time who was meant to live or die, and everyone experienced recurring intimations of his own mortality that day like every other. Yet I felt heartbroken to see my forty-eight-year-old father so utterly despondent, especially after enduring so much together with Gabriel and me since we left home. Which, if either, of our two groups would survive remained a mystery at the moment. But somehow father and sons must have sensed then that they would never see each other again.

7.
Approaching the End

The very day of that fateful selection process, Gabriel and I, together with about a thousand other prisoners, crowded into cattle cars headed out of camp. Once again, now for the fourth time, I was riding that lone train track at Buchenwald, an image that still haunts me. On June 18, we had arrived on that track from Auschwitz. Subsequently, we traveled round trip on it to and from Zeitz. Our December 13, 1944, departure from Buchenwald became our final transit. Without Father's presence and with no word of encouragement from anyone, I felt alone as the train pulled away from Buchenwald's bleak gate. Yet this train trip seemed like the beginning of the end. Rumors had started circulating around camp that the Third Reich was under attack and retreating on both its eastern and western fronts. Surely the war could not last much longer.

Traveling for the first time without Father, Gabriel and I felt both sadness and fear. Although unaware of it at the time, we were the only members of our Transylvanian family still alive. My anxiety heightened as I reflected upon our unremitting dreariness, visible deterioration, and constant hunger. Pondering our desperate condition emboldened further thoughts about trying to escape. *How can I shed these inhuman SS guards and fly this cage? Can I count on German civilians to hide me until the war's end?* I searched for answers until the train stopped and interrupted my thoughts. We had arrived at Berga-Elster Concentration Camp, located in eastern Germany not far from the Czechoslovakian border.

Later on the day of our arrival at Berga, the guards assembled us in the square, surrounded as usual by electrified barbed-wire fences. One of the several SS officers guarding our group began to pace back and forth immediately before the front row of prisoners, perhaps fifteen feet from me. As he surveyed us, I caught his eye for a split second and sensed in it a glimmer of sympathy. The next moment the SS officer stopped, looked directly at me, and shouted that I should step to the side of the assembly. Soon about ten others, mostly younger men, joined me in this small group, which he separated from the majority of the prisoners. The SS officer announced that our small group was assigned to work in the camp's kitchen. Then he ordered us to march directly to the kitchen, just off to our left. As it turned out, this KP detail saved both my life and Gabriel's.

The kitchen was a small room within a wooden barrack. There our group sat on boxes laid out in a semicircle and located about three or four feet from the large hundred-gallon kettles of simmering soup. All day long I sat peeling potatoes. Every morning, as I reported for KP duty, Gabriel and the other prisoners trudged off in columns, under close guard, to hard labor in the nearby mountains. Along with the rest of his large work detail, Gabriel dug out a series of tunnels. I later learned that in these tunnels the Germans secretly intended to rebuild the Brabag gasoline factory destroyed in Zeitz by Allied bombing. Each evening I waited in the yard near the kitchen, which was located only a few feet from the camp's main entrance, for Gabriel's group to return from their day's work in the tunnels. Following dinner, we went to sleep in the bunks within the camp dormitory.

Compared to Auschwitz and Buchenwald with their large number of buildings, Berga was small and makeshift, with two smaller sheds and a single large dormitory. One of the two sheds covered wooden toilets and the other housed the camp's partially enclosed showers. The large dormitory was perhaps once a factory and had a very high ceiling. It consisted of a single large room filled from floor to ceiling and from wall to wall with wooden bunk beds. Eight to ten bunks were stacked about fifteen feet high, row upon row. The top bunks presented a serious climb for an emaciated prisoner, especially after an exhausting day digging tunnels. We slept lined up like so many shoes on a rack.

Notwithstanding its small size, probably not more than fifty square yards, Berga contained a prisoner population of about fifteen hundred men. Consequently, there was little room to move around, and everyone else's misery became one's own. Exacerbating matters further, Berga was experiencing a lice infestation. Despite the bitterly cold winter of 1944–45, many prisoners returning from work sat on the ground with their shirts off, picking out lice. I often did this myself to relieve the terrible itching from colonies of biting lice hidden in the creases of my shirt and pants. Some days, to counteract the lice infestation, the guards sprayed us with DDT. Other days we went untreated, left nitpicking our way to relief. To ease the chronic itching, I took numerous cold showers in Berga's semi-enclosed bathhouse. The bathhouse floor was frigid cement. Yet the ice water that sprayed from overhead pipes offered a welcome, if temporary, relief from the ever-present lice.

Near the bathhouse was the latrine, which was in constant use. It consisted of three or four holes cut out of the top of a long wooden box that ran the length of the wooden shed. Every day people lined up in front of the shed awaiting their turn to get relief from dysentery, a major cause of weakness and death at Berga. And every day, many prisoners died from disease and starvation.

Once, I encountered a man in his fifties who sat on the ground at Berga, bent over sobbing. He had lost his entire family, and without them he had lost all hope. He died soon after. It seemed to me that the cause of his death was as much the psychological impact of his family's loss as the physiological toll of camp life.

Unlike the other camps, Berga did not immediately remove dead bodies. Instead, corpses lay about the camp in plain view for long periods. There they remained, exactly where the prisoners had died, whether in their bunks or the open square. Some men lay dead on the ground outside; others sat propped up against the building. A few seemed ready to expire at any moment, literally almost dead on their feet. Death was omnipresent at Berga.

The constant mortality confounded the daily head counts. At morning head counts, we routinely discovered prisoners who had died in their bunks during the night. The guards counted the prisoners in the camp's assembly square, or *apels platz*, twice daily, once early in the morning before work and once later at night after work but before dinner. First the capos took the count, and then the SS guards repeated it. In the counting process, as with most camp routines, the SS had the capos do their dirty work. On many evenings, the SS guards repeated the count several times, either because of counting errors or because of shortfalls in the number of prisoners. The shortfalls resulted primarily from the recurrent deaths at Berga, but also from sporadic escapes. When the capos and SS could not account for every prisoner, we might stand in line for hours, without food, until the SS was satisfied.

One evening after returning to camp, Gabriel could barely walk even the few feet from the camp entrance to the dormitory out of exhaustion and hunger. As he sat listlessly on the ground outside the dormitory, I stole into the kitchen, which was only ten to twenty yards across a small courtyard. I ladled soup into a metal bowl from one of the large kettles and hurried back across the courtyard to Gabriel with the bowl hidden under my jacket. I stood by him as he quickly ate the soup and soon started feeling better.

We repeated this ritual over several evenings, even though taking soup was a capital offense and the kitchen and dormitory were close to the camp perimeter, which SS guards patrolled constantly, guns at the ready. If caught with the soup, Gabriel and I would have been either hanged or shot—the usual punishment for theft. Nevertheless, I felt surprisingly confident of my ability to go unnoticed to and from the kitchen carrying the bowl of soup. Generally we could do little to help one another, but even this small act had real value. It saved Gabriel's life and bolstered my self-confidence. I watched with satisfaction as Gabriel gradually grew stronger.

One morning, standing by the kitchen entrance near the camp gate, I observed a small, bedraggled contingent of uniformed US soldiers, some of them wearing Red Cross armbands. They came to our camp to collect soup for their fellow military prisoners in their adjacent camp. Several other kitchen workers and I carried thirty- to forty-liter containers of soup to the gate and handed them to the waiting GIs. They carried off the containers of soup without a word exchanged between us. Thereafter, they came by our camp frequently for soup.

After the war, I learned from a documentary made by Charles Guggenheim that these American soldiers were Jews captured in France during the Battle of the Bulge. Because they were Jews or looked Jewish, the SS had segregated them from the other captured GIs and interned them in a concentration camp rather than a POW camp. Typical of their nonadherence to the Geneva Conventions, the Nazis inflicted upon these captured Jewish-American soldiers the same mistreatment visited upon noncombatant European Jews.

At Berga, the SS guards came mostly from countries bordering Russia, like Latvia, Lithuania, and Ukraine. In addition to patrolling the camp perimeter, these Eastern European SS guards stood sentry in a wooden booth at the camp gate through which prisoners went out to work each morning and returned each evening. These SS generally remained outside the electrified fence, except to conduct inspections or to cause mischief. Their internal visits were always dangerous affairs, usually an occasion to brutalize some hapless prisoner. I took pains to avoid them.

One wall of the large dormitory faced the street, and its proximity to the street enabled several prisoners to escape at night into Germany. They ascended the dormitory roof, let themselves down over the fence onto the street below, and fled. Escape was dangerous, however, and few dared try it. Most escapees were caught and promptly hanged or shot. Such was the established lore of the camps reported by older inmates held captive since the late 1930s. Those few who were not caught, we suspected, were aided by ethnic guards who were from their same country. I regularly overheard these guards communicating through the fence in their native language with their countrymen. This national relationship probably saved a Ukrainian prisoner who worked with me in the kitchen. One day he did not show up for work, and we assumed that he had vanished with the aid of Ukrainian camp guards.

To escape was one thing, but to remain free was quite something else. Survival on the run seemed impossible for us Jews. Where would we hide? What would we eat? Who would shelter us? At train station stops en route between camps, I observed German police checking the identity cards of people standing on the platforms. This happened on the glass-covered station platform at Dresden, where our train stopped for the locomotive to take on water en route to Buchenwald. Thus, even if somehow I succeeded in escaping the camp, the prospect of remaining hidden and subsisting thereafter in Germany without civilian support seemed impossible. Moreover, if caught, which seemed likely, I would be killed for sure. Therefore, while I longed to break out, I considered the undertaking to be suicidal. These risk-benefit thoughts preoccupied me day and night.

Intermittently during the early months of 1945, we heard artillery fire in the distance coming from the northeast in the direction of Poland.

During the head count one day, the explosions sounded so close that they drew everyone's attention, including the German guards. Rumors began circulating around the camp that the Russian army was fighting its way through Poland to Berlin in the north and eventually would turn south toward Berga. One April morning, as the explosions from the front became even louder, the guards ordered us to assemble in the yard. By then we had been at Berga for four months. I had no idea that this was to be our last day there.

As we stood at attention that morning, lined up in rows, the camp commandant paced before us accompanied by several SS guards. His name, I later learned, was Willy Hack. He was tall, wore high black boots, and held a whip that he slapped intermittently on the side of his right boot. Commandant Hack announced that he was taking us to a "better place"—his exact words. His voice was mellow, not the usual loud bark that regularly accompanied SS orders. Indeed, throughout my entire camp experience, I had never heard an SS officer talk to us so softly.

I will always remember his words that day: "You do not have to worry, because I am taking care of you. I have provided for your rations so that you will not be hungry on the road." Listening that day to Commandant Hack, I thought to myself that this SS officer had suddenly become human. Instead of treating us harshly, like vile criminals, he planned to care for us decently, like innocent people. Here finally was an SS officer making a promise that he intended to keep—or so I thought. Previously, all SS promises were utter deceptions, designed to induce compliance with their secret and nefarious plans. Naïve belief in such false promises had caused us to behave like sheep, first handing over our property and then our lives. Nothing thus far, however, had prepared me for what was to come. This promise by Hack, like all the other SS promises before it, proved to be bald-faced lie. I discovered this during the march that began the next day.

8.
Head of the Line

On the morning of April 12, 1945, the day following the commandant's address, the SS guards ordered the prisoners to form a long column, the usual five abreast. Presumably this formation was easier for the guards to keep count of us in the march that was to follow. We walked out of the camp with one guard every twenty yards or so on either side of the column. On this day, our guards were new. They were mostly older men, probably in their forties or fifties, but definitely much older than typical SS camp guards. It surprised me to see only one guard for perhaps every fifty prisoners. Though imbalanced, this guard-to-prisoner ratio sufficed; the guards had loaded guns and our condition was weak and dehumanized. Thus began our long death march west from Berga through the German countryside and into the mountains of Sudetenland.

We marched wearing the same wooden shoes given to us upon our arrival in Auschwitz. They bruised our feet and made walking extremely difficult. Although it was biting cold that April, we wore only our usual thin, striped pajama-type pants and shirt, plus a hat of the same material. By contrast, our guards wore thick pants, jackets, and overcoats. Each guard carried a rifle and a backpack containing food; some also packed a revolver. As we set out, each prisoner received a small piece of bread and a slice of margarine. On certain days thereafter, we received watery soup and imitation coffee. On many days, however, we received no food at all. Furthermore, even on those days when we were fed, the meager diet was wholly inadequate to sustain an interminable march in freezing cold weather over mountainous terrain. To exacerbate matters, the guards forced a brisk pace. "Keep moving. Stay in line," they reiterated, while periodically threatening us with their rifles. The march wore everyone down, and every day many died along the way.

Although I became gradually weaker, fear kept me up at the head of the line, with Gabriel following a few paces behind me. At the front of the column, I felt more in touch with what was happening. I could hear the orders as they were barked out from the front and was better able to react. As the march dragged on, the column stretched out. I did not want to find myself in the rear with those having to run periodically in order to catch up, especially now that I was so weak. The feeble, the sick, and the dying trailed at the rear. Occasionally shots rang out from the back of the column. A guard explained the gunfire to me: "Those who don't keep up are shot." This warning confirmed my instinct to remain up front.

Everything I carried seemed an unbearable weight—the clothes, the shoes, even the piece of bread. At night we slept without covers on frozen ground in the fields and forests, except for one evening toward the end of our march when they led us into a barn—but more about that later. Throughout our two-week eastward march over the mountainous German and Sudeten countryside, I never saw any local citizens. Either they kept out of our way and within their houses, or I was too preoccupied with hunger, cold, and survival to notice.

Sitting down was not permitted while on the march. We could rest only when the guards permitted the column to stop, and that seldom happened. Over the course of the march, the guards fed us less and less, and my hunger grew and grew. Eventually my hunger became unbearable. I began eating every type of grass and leaf around, but most of these were either too bitter or too hard to chew. I even tried eating eggshells scattered about a farmyard where we stayed one night. If the egg was edible, I thought, the shell should be too. But once chewed, the shell acquired the texture and provided the nourishment of sand, so I spit it out.

One evening we stopped to rest in a field with a nearby house and barn. Close to dusk, the guards suddenly began yelling and ordered us into a semicircle. They dragged three people to a spot in front of us—a father, his son, and a third person—with their hands tied behind their backs. A farmer had caught them stealing bread inside his home and handed them over to the guards. Either Polish or Lithuanian, the three prisoners were long-time internees. Displaying no emotion, they stood silently before us, side by side, with their heads bowed. Suddenly several shots rang out and all three fell to the ground, dead. After enduring years of camp brutality, they had forfeited their lives for a piece of bread.

We glanced warily at each other and quickly dispersed. I felt sorry for the three victims. But I must admit that at the time, I was thinking primarily of my own survival and simply felt relief at still being alive. Self-preservation remained my dominant concern, especially since I could do nothing to help the three of them. I wonder now how that farmer ever came to terms with having caused those senseless deaths.

Staying alive required constant vigilance, and avoiding run-ins with the guards was key. These old men seemed crazed and ready to kill without provocation. During one stretch, the march followed a serpentine road up to a mountaintop. At various twists and turns in the road, I looked back down toward the end of our long column, which stretched out along the mountainside way below me. I could see some prisoners walking very slowly with the guards next to them, and dead bodies in the road or in roadside ditches where they had fallen.

I wondered where these older German guards were from and what made them so brutal, especially since they looked less intimidating than the younger SS guards who oversaw our four camps (if such a comparison is even meaningful). Perhaps they got this special guard detail because they were local police too old to serve in the military. Throughout the march, their backs and heads remained bent forward with age. Yet they trudged on with a dogged determination. They seemed to know where we were headed, but they never specified our destination and left us to speculate about it in fear.

During our many days on the march through the mountains, we never entered a town center or saw a town name. At one location, I could see a few homes high in the nearby mountains. That same day, it began to snow. At nightfall, our guards arranged with a local farmer to lock us up inside his hay barn. By then, the day's snowfall had soaked through our clothes. We all were wet and shivering. Of the approximately one thousand prisoners who began this march, by now less than half remained alive. The guards jammed us inside the barn for the night—less out of concern for our welfare, I am sure, than for concealing our dead and dying from the local citizens. It also served their needs. One guard could stand sentry duty at the barn entrance and relieve the other guards of standing night watch, as they normally did when we camped in the open.

The farmer's barn was so small that, once forced inside, the remaining five hundred or so of us had no room to sit. We were packed like sardines, with people literally piling on top of one another in search of somewhere to rest. Once the barn door was closed, my cramped situation appeared desperate. I looked around for some secure location free of people for fear of being crushed or trampled to death. There was no space on the ground, but above our heads I noticed the wooden beams holding up the barn roof. Quickly I climbed up onto a beam, several feet over everyone's head, and lay down on it for the night. Looking over the shivering mass of wet people cramped below, I felt a momentary relief from the crowd and began to reminisce about my similar experience at Auschwitz, sleeping alone over the ditch rather than squeezing into one of the bunk beds packed with people all around and above me.

Although occasionally awakened by fear of losing balance on my precarious perch, I still managed to take short naps throughout the night. Gabriel somehow survived the night compressed in the dense mass of humanity below. In the morning, when the barn door opened, I slid down from my perch and proceeded outside in clothes still wet from the prior day's snowfall. Stepping over the prostrate bodies of those who had died in the night, I began to feel anxious about my own ability to endure much more.

While stretching outdoors, thankful at having survived the night, I was pleasantly surprised to find large pots of hot chicory coffee waiting by the barn door. As I drank the coffee from a metal plate (they had no cups), I noticed that some of the guards were talking to occupants of a nearby house who had come outside to observe our gathering. Inside the house, I could see others staring at us through the window from behind little white curtains. The window curtains reminded me of my long-lost domestic tranquility among normal people. Our old guards, by contrast, seemed abnormal, utterly depraved, and devoid of feeling.

Rarely did the civilians living along our march show their faces, and when they did, they usually avoided looking at us directly. One onlooker, however, did stare at us. Shaking his head in dismay, he declared, "*So yung und shon ein verbrecher*" ("So young and already a robber"). Obviously, the guards had reported to the local population that we were criminals. The very idea seemed incredible to me since so many of us were mere youngsters and unlikely villains. Throughout the march, as well as in the camps, whenever I saw any civilians, I had this powerful urge to scream, "We are all innocent people!" I wanted everyone to know that we were guiltless victims of rank injustice, and our prison clothes and skeletal appearance were undeserved and cruel punishment.

Shortly after we exited the barn that morning, the guards assembled us in the usual five-abreast formation. Then we began the day's march along the roadway, periodically ducking into the woods to avoid fire from Allied planes targeting nearby military vehicles. I secretly prayed that some pilot would recognize our plight and selectively pick off our guards, but of course, that was only wishful thinking. Since we had no maps, radios, or newspapers, and the guards told us nothing, we had no idea where we were or where we were going. Even the guards eventually seemed uncertain of their route. It became increasingly apparent, moreover, that they had no specific destination and their real goal was to march us until we all eventually dropped dead from hunger and exhaustion.

At one point our column crossed the border from the Sudeten into Czechoslovakia, and we passed a road sign marking the town of Manetin. At the Czech border, we confronted no crossing guard. None was necessary—Germany had controlled Czechoslovakia since its 1939 invasion. That afternoon, on April 23, 1945, we walked into Manetin. The town was unlike anything we had experienced in the Sudetenland. The people of Manetin stood outside on the street and actually looked at us as our column wended its way into town.

The guards herded us through a large gate into the courtyard and up the stairs of a vacant three-story apartment building that faced directly onto the street. We slept for the night on the bare floors of empty rooms on the building's second and third levels. As I looked down onto the courtyard from the terrace of my room, I could see our guards walking below and talking to one another. No guards stayed the night among us inside the building. Instead, they stood watch by the gate at the building's entrance.

The second day after we arrived in Manetin, Gabriel instructed me to get ready to run away with him. Our situation appeared less tense and less supervised than usual. Indeed, for the first time in a year, our surroundings seemed civilized. The people of Manetin appeared interested and sympathetic, and we saw no guards in the building courtyard or at its rear exit. Furthermore, behind the building was a pasture leading into woods. This unusual setting seemed to present a genuine opportunity to flee captivity. Escape seemed possible, even easy. Gabriel and I walked down the steps of the apartment building, crossed the small center courtyard into a little vegetable garden, and entered the pasture behind the property. Then we started to run.

Gabriel ran in front and I followed for about fifty yards. Suddenly church bells started to ring, signaling 12:00 noon. This meant that the guards were distributing lunch back at the building—maybe soup accompanied by a small piece of bread and margarine. I was starved, and my attention now focused entirely upon food. I abruptly stopped and told Gabriel that I was going back. Without waiting for his response, I turned tail and raced toward the apartment building, thinking only of the awaiting food. Gabriel chased after me, shouting for me to stop, but I could not. We reentered the courtyard now crowded with prisoners. Fortunately, the milling crowd was too numerous for the guards to notice our return. Gabriel was understandably outraged. I had just squandered our first real opportunity in a year to escape. Amazingly, I had chosen captivity over freedom, out of starvation.

As we mingled in the yard, Gabriel, still furious with me, declared angrily, "Hereafter you're on your own. I'm making my escape alone." The next morning, the guards ordered all the prisoners into the street, lined us up five to a row, and headed the column back out of town in the very same direction from which we had entered Manetin. We were returning to the Sudetenland! Suddenly I became terrified. Had I just sacrificed my last chance to escape these Nazis for a mere bowl of soup and piece of bread?

This time, on the highway, I slowly drifted back toward the rear of the column, looking for an opportunity to slip into the woods. Despite our shrinking ranks, reduced significantly even during our brief stay in Manetin, Gabriel and I became separated in the line of prisoners and eventually lost sight of each other. As we passed the sign at the outskirts of Manetin, I realized that I could no longer see any of our guards. Quickly I walked off the road and hid myself behind the wide base of a large statue of Christ nailed to a wooden cross.

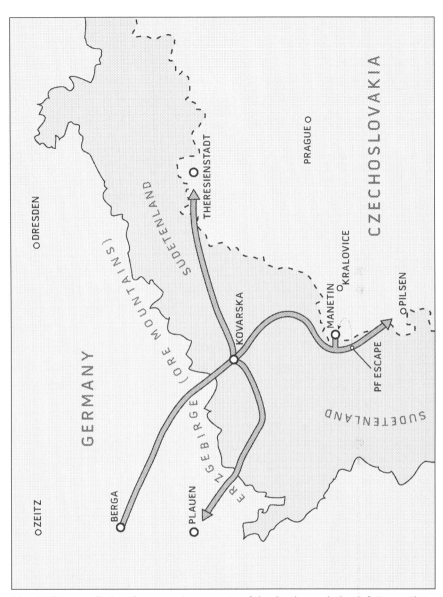

Map 6: This map depicts the approximate route of the death march that left Berga-Elster Concentration Camp on April 12, 1945, proceeding east through Sudetenland over the Erzgebirge (Ore Mountains) and into Czechoslovakia. We spent a night at a barn located in Kovarska after which (unbeknownst to us at the time) the guards separated the marchers into three groups: one headed east to Theresienstadt, another west to Plauen, and ours south to Manetin, Czechoslovakia. We arrived in Manetin on April 23 and left on April 28, proceeding south back into Sudetenland and heading toward Pilsen. As we reentered Sudetenland, I escaped and returned to Manetin by circling around to the south and reentering it from the east.

Built on an elevated shoulder about five yards away from the road, the cross stood inside a small garden surrounded by a low wooden fence. I planned to shield myself behind the cross until all the prisoners and guards had passed on down the road. If I were discovered there, I had readied an explanation for the guards: I needed to go to relieve myself. But eventually, fearing that the guards might still see me at this location, I stood up from behind the cross and walked away from the highway through an empty field toward a distant forest where I could hide more safely.

I had not walked more than seventy-five yards when I heard a sharp whistle behind me on the highway. Ignoring the whistle, I walked on, while at the same time fearing that any moment a bullet would strike me in my back. Upon hearing a second whistle, I turned around and saw a guard standing on the road below alongside his bicycle. He aggressively motioned me back to the highway. Immediately I retraced my steps to the road. When I reached the highway, the guard yelled his displeasure and angrily waved me on toward the column, which by now was far out of sight in front of us. The guard then climbed back on his bicycle and pedaled ahead, expecting that I would follow along with the few remaining stragglers. I felt lucky that he had not shot me. But I also felt a return of my self-confidence very nearly destroyed in the camps.

Soon my small group crossed the border from Czechoslovakia back into Sudetenland. Anxious about proceeding any further into German territory and seeing very few prisoners nearby, I searched for another chance to slip away and head back into Czechoslovakia. I could not see Gabriel and knew I had to go on alone. Just beyond the Czech border, we crossed a small bridge where I regained my courage. Hopping over a trench along the left side of the road, I ran through a field toward a forest off in the distance and never looked back. For the first time since leaving Hadad, I felt the exhilaration of freedom and shed much of the fear that had suffocated me for almost a year.

Running past the only house in that field, I saw a woman peeking out from behind a curtain. She stared at me for a second and then closed the curtain. I ran on and again became frightened. Would she report my escape to the Germans? This fear sped me on faster up the hills until I had left the Sudetenland behind and entered the Czech forest. I was circling

Manetin on the south, heading east, and plunging headlong through the surrounding trees. As darkness descended, I could see the lights of Manetin to my left in the valley below. I had to avoid recapture or surely they would execute me on the spot. Already on the run and so close to freedom, I had little to lose by racing onward. There was no living soul in sight. That too was a problem, however; I needed some Czech citizen to hide and feed me.

After more than an hour without stopping, I regained confidence that at long last I had really and truly escaped. By this point I had reached the east side of Manetin, with Czechoslovakia spread out before me and Germany far behind, receding into the distance with my every step. Alone for the first time in almost one year, I became afraid. Crossing a road that led into town from the east, I approached a house and knocked on the door. To my shock and gratitude, the Czech woman who answered the door invited me in. I entered into a dark room. She motioned me to turn right, and I walked through a doorway into the kitchen. It was empty except for a table with a bench on either side and two or three blankets laid out on the floor like beds. Looking around the kitchen, I was startled to see two strange and frightened men standing there staring at me. Instantly it became apparent that they too were escapees. I wondered where they had come from and how they had gotten here. Were they from Berga with my group? But this was no time for questioning. Furthermore, they came from some Slavic country, so we did not speak the same language. Instead, we only exchanged glances. More to the point, we all were starved and must have looked it, since our kind hostess placed a bowl of soup and a piece of bread on the table before each of us.

I felt secure in the company of this Czech woman. At last I had found a decent human being willing to help me. For the first time since being taken prisoner by the Germans, someone—an utter stranger—was actually taking care of me. What a miracle! We ate the soup and bread hurriedly and without conversation. Then in broken German, our good Samaritan explained that we needed to leave early in the morning because her house was next to the highway and German guards would likely search it. I slept fitfully on the floor along with the other two men, waking up periodically to listen for any movement outside the house. In the morning she gave each of us another piece of bread. With the bread in hand, the three of us assembled outside. Without any discussion of our plans, we started walking together through the woods beside the main highway toward the center of Manetin.

Several other men soon joined our stealthy roadside movement. I assumed that they were fleeing from the Russian front near Prague. Whenever we saw German cars and motorcycles approaching on the nearby road, we hid behind trees with our hearts pounding, determined never to be recaptured. I had reclaimed my life and would not relinquish it again. As we walked along, I came to a ditch. Another man and I were about to jump over it when we simultaneously noticed paper money lying in the mud. After quickly glancing at one another, we moved on toward town without stopping to pick up the money, implicitly agreeing that it held no interest for us. Life was far more precious than money, which had ceased to have meaning. If we were caught while escaping, the money surely would not buy our freedom. Quite the opposite—it would seal our fate as thieves.

Eventually we reached the center of Manetin, where some local people guided us to the main high-school building not far from where Gabriel and I attempted our abortive escape a few days earlier. I will never forget the kindness and warmth of these Czech people. A school official had us sit on chairs in a classroom awaiting the townspeople who slowly gathered at the school. Each Czech family agreed to hide one prisoner until the war was over. My sponsoring family, a woman and her daughter, lived on the main street not far from the school. They clothed, fed, and cared for me as if I were one of their own. After being locked up for almost a year, guarded like a wild animal, and living in constant fear of death, I felt strangely disoriented in this family setting. It was hard to comprehend. I was suddenly free and once again enjoying normal domestic comforts. Every day from the darkened living room of the house I cautiously peered out the window from behind the curtains at German soldiers retreating west along the road toward the Sudetenland, terror written over their faces. This role reversal felt incredibly gratifying. Now the Germans were the hunted.

While hiding with the family in Manetin, I developed a high fever. The family was so caring that they brought me to a hospital in the nearby town of Kralovice, where I was diagnosed with pneumonia. The cause was probably our day's march in the snow and my night sleeping aloft in the barn rafters in thin wet clothes. Now I faced another life challenge—surviving a serious respiratory illness in my debilitated condition—but as a free man.

My parents, Morice and Ida Frenkel, in 1933, with Gabriel sitting on the sled behind four-year-old me. In the background is our first house in Hadad, where I lived from birth until age eight (1929–1937).

A 1936 photo with Gabriel in the foreground holding his pants, Joska Richter sitting on the donkey at the very back, and me sitting in the middle directly in front of him.

My elementary schoolmates in Hadad in about 1937, when I was eight years old. I am circled top center, and my boyhood friend Joska Richter is circled lower left.

A 1937 photo of my cousin Judith, myself, and my mother, Ida, taken in Szamosujvar near the Armenian church where I sang in the choir.

Mihaly Bacsi, horse caretaker for Count Banfi, in about 1944.

The front façade of Banfi Castle today.

Hadad in a picture taken during my 1987 family visit. It shows the main street looking east toward Szilagy Cseh, with residences on either side, the steeple of the Reformed Church, and the gate to the church immediately to the right of the horse cart. The electric and telephone poles substantially postdate our departure from Hadad in April 1944.

Pigs heading home in 1987, reminiscent of what I saw when I lived in Hadad in the early 1940s.

Hodod's main well for drinking and washing water, with an adjacent trough to water cattle and horses. On the pole next to the well is a stork's nest, a common sight in Hodod.

The front entrance to what was Grandmother Cili Frenkel's textile shop in Gherla, Romania, with two windows and a center entrance door. Peasants bought Grandmother's textiles to make their clothes at home. In 1987, her shop had become an electronic store, with a butcher shop next door.

A **1943** photo of the Frenkel family taken in Szamosujvar, showing Gabriel, Ida, Morice, and me.

My grandparents Cili and Morton Frenkel at about age seventy-two and seventy-five in the picture taken about 1943 in Szamosujvar, then part of Hungary.

Tracks leading to the entrance of Auschwitz where, starting in mid-1942, the Nazis killed the largest numbers of European Jews, including my parents, grandparents, and aunt, by gassing with Zyklon-B.

The infamous sign above the gate in Auschwitz reading "Arbeit Macht Frei," which means "Work Makes You Free."

This is one page of the manifest of June 18, 1944, from Auschwitz to Buchenwald, listing my father, Morice (53998), my brother, Gabriel (54000), and me (53999). These were the personal numbers given us upon our initial arrival at Buchenwald. The manifest shows us as numbers 178, 179, and 180 among the prisoners transported that day by cattle car.

701	97417	Z.	Fischer, R.	751	53091	23	Seleser, S.
702	480		Rottmann, A.	752	53999		Trenkel,
703	496		Landemann, P.	753	54000		Frenkel, G.
704	535		Guttmann, A.	754	56750		Spira
705	562		Löwith, A.	755	57357		Jlovits,
706	622		Singer, W.	756	57377		Fridmann, A.
707	756		Györi, M.	757	57454		Todol, S.
708	763		Perl, L.	758	57938		Lewkovits,
709	98033		Pavlovics, A.	759	58182		Steinitz, L.
710	100		Fedkiv, M.	760	58545		Löwinger,
711	203		Kuzmenko, J.	761	59221		Müller, L.
712	235		Mezenzew, K.	762	59242		Lebavits, A.
713	276		Zacharew, W.	763	64556		Bock, J.
714	287		Klein, R.	764	64718		Kohn, E.
715	304		Ciecerski, W.	765	64725		Heimler, J.
716	513		Raab, Z.	766	64730		Klein
717	532		Kupec, B.	767	64754		Feldmann
718	536		Ponger, V.	768	64817		Friedmann, J.
719	543		Mirsow, A.	769	65625		Klein, J.
720	569		Buschpaj, N.	770	65918		Gottesmann, L.
721	604		Urban, A.	771	66234		Gutmann
722	606		Dowy, N.	772	66315		Glöckner, C.
723	607		Glasel, P.	773	66523		Laubermann, G.
724	611		Ziegler, E.	774	66554		Frenkel, S.
725	618		Rosenbaum, E.	775	66559		Neumann, S.
726	650		Schlossmann	776	66642		Fand, G.
727	654		Plener, M.	777	66777		Müller, P.
728	671		Schubert, Fr.	778	67515		Keil,
729	698		Müller, A.	779	67529		Mazgowski, Ch.
730	709		Steiner, J.	780	67695		Frenkel, J.
731	802		Milchapeiser, A.	781	67698		Braun
732	8959	22	Bock, A.	782	67716		Sztern, N.
733	6336		Scheuer	783	67717		Fajgenbaum, L.
734	52403		Goldmann, M.	784	67872		Feresztendijk, J.
735	52709		Steinberger, A.	785	67909		Markowicz, S.
736	52951		Mosbach, E.	786	68911		Rosenberg, M.
737	55677		Kroh,	787	67998		Holckiener, S.
738	57946		Brandstein, J.	788	68099		Tochtermann, J.
739	58940		Steinberger, D.	789	68133		Ringel
740	65147		Reiszfeld, A.	790	68252		Morowicz,
741	66273		Schwarz, S.	791	68300		Zylberminc, J.
742	67727		Rozental, S.	792	68342		Bernieman, Z.
743	68403		Brzyski, S.	793	68345		Flamenbaum, D.
744	83739		Frenkel, S.	794	68469		Gastfrajnd, Ch.
745	83819		Wroblewski, B.	795	68579		Perel, J.
746	83852		Schklaper, A.	796	68718		Armer, N.
747	83886		Willner, J.	797	68741		Grünberg, B.
748	84609		Wojcol, W.	798	68744		Grünberg, J.
749	53200	23	Weisz,	799	68745		Brünberg, Sz.
750	52684		Weisz, A.	800	68784		Blumen, G.

17035

This is page eight of the ten-page manifest of December 13, 1944, from Buchenwald to Berga, listing my brother Gabriel (54000) and me (53999), with my name misspelled as "Trenkel." We are numbers 752 and 753 among the 1,000 prisoners transported that day by cattle car.

The sign "Jedem Das Seine" on the iron gate at Buchenwald, meaning "To Each His Own."

Picture of Gabriel and me taken upon our reunion in Bucharest, Romania, shortly after our separate escapes from the Berga death march in April 1945.

Uncle Feri Frenkel photographed me standing in the water next to a boat on the Black Sea near Odessa, where Feri took me for a brief vacation in July or August 1945, a few months after my escape from the Berga death march.

Uncle Max and Aunt Margo with their sons Eddy and Nathan, taken in Bucharest, Romania, in 1947.

Uncle Feri in Arad, Romania, in early 1940.

A 1948 photo of police officers of the Neu Freiman displaced persons camp in Munich, Germany. I am carrying the flag.

My coworkers in the dining room for employees of the Joint Distribution Committee in Munich in 1948 (surrounding me in the center). They include the man from Szamosujvar who hired me (third from right) and Fritz Jahleh, with whom I spent my free time while in Munich (second from left).

Picture of me taken aboard the USS *General JHM Rae* en route from Bremerhaven, Germany, to New York City in September 1949.

A **1981** photo of Mihaly Bacsi and his wife standing at the front door of their house in Hodod.

Cutting the ribbon to open my dairy plant at the US Naval Base in Rota, Spain, on July 26, 1981 (I am in the center, second from left).

Plaque memorializing my Distinguished Service Award from Delaware Valley College in Doylestown, Pennsylvania, on May 2, 2009.

A 2002 photo of Rita, Paul, Nick, and Tori taken in the kitchen of our home in New Preston, Connecticut, prior to the arrival of our four grandsons.

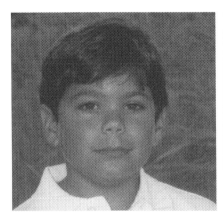

Paul and Rita's grandsons Theo and Simon, sons of Victoria and Thomas.

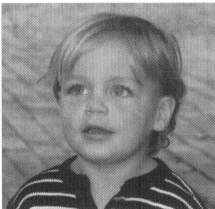

Paul and Rita's grandsons Oliver and Logan, sons of Nicholas and Nanci.

PART III: THE ODYSSEY

Half to forget the wandering and pain,
Half to remember days that have gone by,
And dream and dream that I am home again!

James Elroy Flecker, "Brumana"

9.
Rebuilding in Romania

I stayed at the Kralovice hospital for two weeks in a room with about ten other patients while doctors and nurses treated my pneumonia. The hospital staff knew that I was an escaped prisoner but said nothing to anyone about my identity. A Czech nurse told me to remain quiet so that I would not be discovered. Germans were still fighting Russians and Americans inside Czechoslovakia as the Eastern and Western fronts converged near Pilzen. Watching these concerned doctors and nurses deliver such conscientious patient care reminded me of Father. Where was he now, I worried, and where were Mother and Gabriel?

The hospital staff treated me well, cured my pneumonia, and released me back to the Czech family in Manetin. Upon returning to their home, I resumed my watch over the Germans from behind the curtains in their living-room window. The soldiers continued to flee westward along the main street on foot and horseback, in carts and motor vehicles, holding guns at the ready. Visibly frightened, they peered nervously at buildings on either side of the road as they sped westward. They feared not only the fast-approaching Russians behind them but also the rebellious Czechs around them. The Czechs reportedly had just staged an uprising in Prague, and Czech snipers were harassing the soldiers' retreat into Germany. In fact, my sponsor's son had joined the Czech partisans to fight the Germans.

The last German had barely left Manetin when the Russians flooded into town on horseback, calling out for directions to Berlin. I watched the war front move westward directly before me and felt enormous relief. If only the lingering horror of the camps could be swept away as quickly.

After about two quiet weeks of family life in Manetin, I decided it was safe to return home. The war front had moved west from Czechoslovakia into Germany, and Transylvania was to the southeast. Since I had no identity papers, my host family kindly took me by car to Prague, where the Red Cross issued me a refugee document to present in case I was stopped. Unfortunately, Prague was in turmoil, and the refugee agency could not provide additional help. So I set out to find my own way back to Transylvania. I walked to the Prague railway station, hoping to board a train heading south to the Czech border. There I planned to cross into Hungary, board a train to Budapest, and thence move on to Romania. In both Arad and Bucharest, Romania, I had close relatives—the families of my Uncles Feri and Max Frenkel, respectively. Although I had neither money nor train tickets, I felt renewed self-confidence, certain that my recent good luck had not yet run out. I fully expected to be reunited soon with my parents and brother.

At the Prague station, I befriended a Russian soldier who had gone AWOL. He still wore his long military trench coat and carried a long, heavy rifle with a bayonet. He teamed up with me, thinking that my youthful and innocent appearance would make him less conspicuous to the surrounding Russian forces. He gave me his trench coat, and we walked across the tracks until we found a train going our way and hopped aboard. We traveled as far as Brno, Czechoslovakia, where the train stopped at nightfall, forcing all passengers to disembark. Stuck for the night in this largely deserted train yard, we scrounged for food and slept on the cement floor of the station platform. There we encountered a young girl, no older than me, who begged that we let her sleep between us for the night, possibly because she felt safe with someone her own age. She was frightened speechless because (I suspect) she had been raped by Russian soldiers.

In the morning the girl left us, and the Russian and I resumed our journey toward the Czech border by boarding a train headed south to Bratislava. Once again, to mask his AWOL status, the Russian handed me his rifle and trench coat, which he had taken back the prior evening. At a bombed-out bridge near Bratislava the train came to a stop, leaving us to proceed on foot across the bridge, which had collapsed into the flowing river. We had not gone far beyond the bridge before a Russian military patrol detained the two of us. They took us to military headquarters for questioning, uncovered the Russian's AWOL status, and arrested him. I convinced them that I was a liberated refugee of the Nazi camps, and they let me go, with the rifle still slung over my shoulder.

I boarded another train in Bratislava, crossed the Hungarian border, and eventually arrived at a large passenger terminal in Budapest. A Russian patrol scanned the discharging passengers for illegals, but I avoided them and headed to the street. I looked for a streetcar, intent on finding the home of my father's distant cousin, whom I had never met. The war had wrecked the city, including the famous Chain Bridge over the Danube that connected Buda and Pest. The bridge hung down into the water, forcing me to walk on the submerged steel beam knee-deep in the river to reach Buda, on the other side, where my relatives lived.

Once safely across the river, I boarded a trolley. As the trolley started up, the conductor passed among the passengers and upon reaching me asked for my ticket. Of course I had none, since I was penniless. Nevertheless, I felt allied with my Russian liberators and superior to the defeated Hungarians, who were criminally aligned with the Nazis and primarily responsible for my family's suffering. I confronted the conductor, confidently patting the rifle on my shoulder, and he quickly moved on to the next passenger. Not only was I finally mingling among civilians after a year in captivity, but suddenly I had reacquired a personal identity. I was wearing civilian clothing given me by the family in Manetin—not a striped uniform. I was speaking perfect Hungarian in familiar Hungary—not struggling with the imperfect German in hostile Germany. Furthermore, I was no longer just a number but once again a genuine person. My approach to people was different, more self-confident, but I still remained unsure of exactly who I had become.

After obtaining directions from passersby, I eventually found my relatives' apartment. Fortunately, they had survived the Holocaust along with most of the other Jews in Budapest. The Budapest Jews were about the only Jews in Hungary spared deportation to Auschwitz. My father's cousin and his wife, Suranyi and Rozsika Ference, were elated to see me alive. They welcomed me enthusiastically into their home. For the second time since my liberation, I was with a family in their home. Since the Russian Army occupied Budapest, the Ferences became nervous about my having a Russian rifle. The occupying Russians had outlawed civilian firearms, were hunting down collaborators, and remained justifiably suspicious of all Hungarians. At my relatives' request and to ease their anxiety I followed them to the Russian authorities and turned over the rifle.

After a few days of wandering about Budapest to view the city's devastation, I said good-bye to the Ferences and headed to the railway station, intent on boarding a passenger train bound for Arad, Romania. I thought my parents and Gabriel would likely head either for Arad, where Uncle Feri lived, or for Bucharest, where Uncle Max lived. At the time I knew nothing of the German extermination program and, therefore, remained optimistic about my parents' return. Russian soldiers packed the train standing at the Budapest station and barred Hungarians from boarding. Consequently, I had to talk my way onboard, citing my recent camp experience. My youth and apparent innocence carried the day. The soldiers waved me aboard, leaving all the other civilians stranded on the platform.

The train went as far south as Szeged and stopped, forcing us to get off and wait there until morning for the next train out. The station was badly damaged and afforded no enclosure. Consequently, I spent the night among a large crowd of refugees huddled in the central square that faced the train station. I felt safe within the crowd and lay down near a light pole on the paving stones that covered the square. Since the train station was only half a block away and the tracks were visible from my location, I expected to hear the crowd's early-morning commotion in ample time to catch the first train to Romania. I quickly dozed off to sleep, propping my head on the small bag that contained my ID and some food.

I slept so soundly that by the time I awoke in the morning, the square was deserted. Startled at first to find everyone gone, I was greatly relieved to see the morning train for Romania still waiting at the station and ran to catch it. Once again I had to talk my way aboard and entered a compartment crammed with Russian soldiers. Happily, the conductors on trains operating in Russian-occupied Hungary and Romania did not fuss about passports or tickets.

The train eventually crossed into Romania and stopped just across the border in Arad. Conversant in Romanian as well as Hungarian, I asked about and soon located my relatives' address. Although I had not met them previously, my Uncle Feri, his wife, Piri, and their two daughters, Agi (age nine) and Erica (age six), greeted me with such joy that I will never forget our meeting that day. When my introductory tour of their apartment reached the girls' bedroom, they jumped up and down on their beds in excitement. What an unforgettable welcome!

The next day they took me for a walk through the center of Arad, where we visited distant relatives, an elderly couple with a middle-aged daughter. How strange it was to be among family members completely ignorant of the Nazi camps—wholly unaware of the constant hunger, endless labor, and terrible murders of their fellow Jews. While conversation about ordinary city life was interesting, I found it difficult to adjust to such normalcy after living for almost a year with people obsessed with their very survival. Unburdening myself to them about the horrors of camp life was not easy, and even enjoying my newfound freedom took considerable effort. After leaving these distant relatives, we returned downtown, where Uncle Feri found an ice-cream parlor. He treated all of us to indescribably delicious vanilla ice-cream cones in celebration of my survival.

Tempering my joy over the enthusiastic greeting by Feri's family was my concern that my parents and brother were still missing. I had hoped that by now they would have reached Uncle Feri in Arad. Alternatively, I thought they might have gone directly to see Uncle Max. So, after a week in Arad, I said my good-byes and resumed my train journey to Bucharest. There I hoped to become reunited with my mother, last seen in Auschwitz; my father, separated from us in Buchenwald; and my brother, gone his own way after we left Manetin.

In Bucharest, Uncle Max, his wife, Sidona, daughter Judith, and son Gabriel were relieved to see me. They too happily welcomed me into their apartment, offered me a private room with a comfortable bed, provided me with clean clothes, gave me food aplenty, and even encouraged me to take regular showers. They had a separate kitchen, served food on clean plates, and used knives, forks, and spoons with every meal. This was real luxury. Unfortunately, they had no information to share about my family. Within a few days, however, Gabriel appeared at their door. He had escaped from the death march shortly after leaving Manetin, came looking for me there without success, and then found his way to Bucharest through the American lines. At least we two had survived the camps.

Soon thereafter, Uncle Feri moved his whole family from Arad to Bucharest. But he brought no news of my parents. Feri could see my dejection over the lack of information about my parents, and shortly thereafter he took me on a short vacation. The two of us went by train to

Odessa, where we enjoyed several days together at a beach on the Black Sea (see cover photograph). Uncle Feri tended to my physical as well as my emotional well-being. He rented two small apartments in a building at 8 Dr. Victor Poloni Street in Bucharest, one on the first floor for his family and the other on the top floor for Gabriel and me. Furthermore, he provided us with this apartment rent-free. With financial support from both uncles, Gabriel returned to his studies at university in Bucharest, and I returned to Hadad (now called Hodod) in search of my parents. Hodod held my one remaining hope for their return.

By July 1945, Romania had reasserted control of northern Transylvania, so the familiar names of towns had all changed back once again from Hungarian to Romanian. I arrived by train at Cehu Silvaniei (formerly Szilagy Cseh), walked the seven miles to Hodod, and proceeded directly to our home. It was stripped bare. Everything was gone; the house was empty of all its furniture and personal effects. And my parents were still missing. I went next door to call upon my good friend Joska Richter and his family. To my surprise, the Richters greeted me coldly, confining our brief and strained meeting to their kitchen and grocery store. They never once inquired about my family or mentioned what happened to our home after we were deported. I was surprised by their standoffish behavior and wondered what it meant. They probably had assumed we would never return. Now I was standing before them, and they felt guilty.

Disturbed and disoriented by this chilly reception from such old friends, I left the Richters to seek out my other friends. Moses Adorjan, the former manager of Banfi estate, embraced me, welcomed me back, and put me up for four or five days in a bedroom in his home. I received a similarly warm greeting from Uncle Mihaly, the former Banfi coach driver, and from the pharmacist. Also, when walking up the hill behind the market square one day, I introduced myself to a peasant who remembered me and my father. Otherwise, I was essentially a stranger in town. The Jews were gone. Even the Lutheran minister Aichelin and his family were gone. Quite understandably, considering their ethnicity and apparently collaborative behavior toward the Nazi regime, they had moved to Germany.

Hodod seemed in denial. No one talked about the deportations. No one appeared concerned or spoke to me about the fate of my parents or our Jewish neighbors. For years, my father had been their only family doctor. He had delivered many of them as babies, cured their illnesses, even saved their lives. Yet no one expressed compassion for my parents' suffering or even showed interest in whether they had survived. These former neighbors and friends of ours during my fourteen years growing up in Hodod did not seem to care.

I still cannot fathom their indifference. Perhaps they were embarrassed over their acceptance of (or complicity in) the deportations, or their looting of Jewish homes. Hodod was different, very different, and not just in name. I had become an outsider. Obviously, I could expect no support there. The idyllic town of my childhood had become strangely alien. I departed Hodod with a heavy heart, resigned to never seeing my parents again. Had they survived the camps, my parents certainly would have returned home, but no one had seen them in Hodod. Reluctantly acknowledging their likely fate and my unexpected estrangement from formerly beloved Hodod, I determined to embark on a new life elsewhere.

After returning to Bucharest, I visited the Ministry of Agriculture to inquire about agricultural schools and located one in Tirgu Mures, forty miles southeast of Cluj. I traveled to Tirgu Mures for an interview, applied, and was accepted. The school gave me credit for my gymnasium coursework in Cluj (Kolozsvar) and Gherla (Szamosujvar), which also served me well in my later collegiate career. In the fall of 1945, with financial help from Uncle Max, I began classes. Because food was scarce throughout Romania, the school required me to pay tuition in produce. So following every vacation, I returned to school with a sack of potatoes or other raw produce, like wheat, which Max furnished me money to purchase on the black market in Bucharest or Tirgu Mures.

At the school, I studied farming: sowing fields, raising and harvesting crops (potatoes, beets, watermelon, wheat, and corn), and caring for pigs, horses, and cows. The agricultural school was both structured and spartan. Every day we marched like soldiers from the dormitory near the center of town to the school farm outside the city, about five miles distance. There we practiced traditional farming—nothing yet was motorized. At day's end we returned to the school dormitory, again in military formation.

We slept on straw mattresses laid on the floor in our dormitory rooms, ate bread and lots of corn (a bread substitute and staple of the Romanian diet), and drank water drawn by a single hand pump in the courtyard. The hand pump also served as our communal wash-up facility. This open washroom was comfortable in summer but bracing in winter. Early every morning in every season we walked shirtless into the courtyard to wash our upper body.

While attending school in Tirgu Mures, I inquired at the Jewish Community Center about the young Jewish boy committed to our care by his father in the Little Camp at Buchenwald. I found him living with his mother in a small top-floor apartment located near my school. His mother was heartbroken at the murder of her husband and her daughter at Auschwitz. Since their family meals surpassed the school fare, I visited them almost daily. But our collective mourning over the loss of family members in the Nazi camps cast a pall over every meal.

During school vacations, I traveled to Bucharest by train from Tirgu Mures through Brasov, then up over the Carpathian Mountains and down through Ploesti. Ascending the high Carpathians, the train chugged slowly because of the steep grade and passed through two long tunnels. Usually the Bucharest train was completely full, so the only available space was outside on top. I sat there with my legs hanging down between two cars, facing front. This perch required considerable vigilance. I had to lie back each time the train entered a tunnel in order to avoid hitting my head on its low overhead. Also, to avoid suffocating in the tunnel, I had to hold my breath as the dense smoke drifted back over the passenger cars from the locomotive up front.

At this time, Bucharest itself was becoming dangerous, with frequent, often violent demonstrations against the Communist government staged outside King Carol's palace. I regularly passed the demonstrators when heading on foot or by trolley to our apartment or when visiting the palace square out of sheer curiosity. Suddenly the police would descend upon the palace and start shooting into the crowd. People scattered for their lives.

Despite the surrounding political turmoil, Uncle Max led an orderly and prosperous life. He owned a small factory that manufactured machine parts for the Romanian army. His chauffeur pulled up to his home punctually each morning at 8:10 a.m. and drove off with Max to the bank so that he could withdraw newly printed banknotes needed for the day's business. Then his chauffeur transported him from one client to another. Max returned home every noon for lunch and a brief nap. At exactly 3:05 p.m., the chauffeur reappeared, ready to transport him to his afternoon round of meetings. Uncle Max expected the same exactitude from Gabriel and me, requiring that we prepare a detailed accounting of how we spent every penny that he gave us for school and living expenses. Gabriel objected to Max's terms, but I accepted them uncomplainingly. Later in life I applied them in my own business affairs, requiring the same careful accounting from my employees.

Uncle Feri also was a businessman, but he was a speculator and entrepreneur rather than an industrialist like Uncle Max. Feri bought oranges from Palestine and vegetables from other European countries, imported them into Romania after paying the required import duty and unavoidable bribes, and then sold them for profit on the Romanian market. Periodically I accompanied Feri in his chauffeur-driven car to observe his trading in agricultural commodities. On one occasion I carried a sackful of paper money to pay for a railcar load of oranges that he had imported from Palestine. Both uncles lived well.

After three years attending agricultural school in Tirgu Mures, I stood at the top of my class academically. At winter break in early 1948, during my final year before graduation, Gabriel received a prearranged call from the United States in our Bucharest apartment. My mother's brother, Uncle David Ince (he changed his name from Israel), called to urge Gabriel and me to emigrate to the United States. Uncle David, his two brothers, Ernest and Eugene, and his sister, Nellie, had emigrated to the United States before the war, in the 1930s. Anticipating a rewarding career in Romanian agriculture, I initially resisted the unexpected offer. But Gabriel thought otherwise. He badly wanted to go to the United States, and ultimately convinced me that we had no real future in Romania. Given its current political turmoil, economic distress, and Communist orientation, I had to concur. So we both accepted the invitation and prepared immediately to leave Romania.

Uncle David advised that we apply for a US visa in the nearest and most accessible non-Communist country. That was Germany, which presented a problem. To reach the American zone in Germany, we needed to travel from Romania through the Russian zones in Hungary and Austria. Our target destination in Germany was the Bavarian city of Munich.

With help from uncles Max and Feri, Gabriel and I devised a plan. Uncle Feri offered to take us on the first leg of our journey by train from Bucharest to Arad, his former home. There he would find someone to take us across the border to the nearest railroad station inside Hungary. Once inside Hungary we could catch a train to Budapest, where we would make connections with Jewish organizations to transport us to Vienna, then to Salzburg, and from there to Munich.

After we reached Arad and waited a couple of days there, Uncle Feri rode with us to the local railroad station in a horse-drawn taxi. As Gabriel and I boarded the train headed for the Hungarian border, Feri gave us a wad of Hungarian, Austrian, and German currency to see us through to Munich. We bade him farewell, never imagining that our paths would cross again under better circumstances on another continent.

After the train pulled out of Arad, the Romanian conductor took and punched our tickets but then hesitated to return them. He kept looking quizzically at the two of us and then at the tickets. Finally he said there was a problem with our tickets that might prevent us from continuing on the train. He needed to call the police to check out the purpose of our trip. Gabriel and I began to panic. Then the conductor offered to resolve the problem privately among the three of us. Knowing that bribes were the *modus operandi* in Romania, we offered him a "fee." He promptly accepted our gratuity, returned our tickets, and let us proceed to our destination without further ado. We got off the train at a small Romanian station located at the Hungarian border.

Next, the plan called for us to proceed at night on foot across farmland adjoining the two countries. Once on the Hungarian side of the border, we would walk to the nearby train station and board the early morning train for Budapest. To reach the train station within Hungary during the night was itself an adventure. We could not have made it without help from the guide prearranged by Uncle Feri. Immediately after leaving the train we found our contact, who took us by horse carriage to a field at the border. After nightfall our guide led us on foot across the border in pitch dark. We hid in bushes to avoid detection by the intermittent Hungarian border patrols. By daybreak, we had reached the Hungarian train station where our guide left us to catch the first passenger train to Budapest.

Opening the door to the station, I saw a policeman standing inside at the ticket window. To avoid him we immediately withdrew and circled around behind the station. Luckily, the train was already at the station and ready to leave. So we quickly boarded, intending to buy our tickets onboard. We had no trouble doing so since we spoke Hungarian and carried Hungarian money. Uncle Feri had shown great foresight in giving us Hungarian currency for just such an eventuality. We made it to Budapest without incident and stayed overnight with a charitable organization.

Fortunately for us, many Jewish refugees wanted to emigrate from Europe to Palestine, which was in turmoil in 1948. The Jewish agency in Budapest had an elaborate network for shuttling Jews across European borders into Italy and then east across the Mediterranean to fight for the new Jewish state of Israel. Assuming that Gabriel and I were aspiring Israeli patriots, the Jewish network arranged to transport us by truck from Budapest to Vienna along with a group of other Romanian refugees. Since both cities were in the Russian zone, we proceeded easily out of Hungary and into eastern Austria. At the Austrian border, another guide met us and drove us directly to the Jewish agency in Vienna. The agency put us up for the night and arranged for an experienced driver to transport us the next day by canvas-covered truck into the American zone.

Densely packed with three rows of refugees lining the full length of the vehicle, our covered truck passed through Vienna's four occupied zones heading toward Salzburg. On this trip I saw blinking traffic lights and stop signs for the first time—my introduction to the industrialized West. Just as we exited the city of Vienna, an armed Russian roadblock stopped and searched our truck. Flipping open the back flap, the Russian soldier barked, "Where do you think you're going?" He ordered us out of the truck. Since only Gabriel and I spoke Hungarian, we sat at the very back and assumed responsibility for addressing the Russian soldiers.

Our purpose in speaking Hungarian was to mask everyone's Romanian identity. We offered up an innocuous explanation about our group and its destination—and apparently an unconvincing one, since the explanation failed to relieve the Russians' suspicions about us. Instead, they walked us all to a nearby station and sent us by train under guard back into the center of Vienna. As angry as we were about this turn of events, Gabriel and I remained silent for fear of antagonizing the Russians.

At the very first station stop, we redressed our unexpected setback. To the consternation of our single Russian guard, we all simultaneously got up and promptly exited the train. The guard stood by dumbfounded. There were too many of us for him to stop as the train began to pull out of the station toward Vienna. Once off the train, we set out briskly on foot toward the highway leading back to where we had left the truck. Along the way, the men took turns comforting the women in our group. By this point, they were crying inconsolably for fear of being caught.

Luckily our guide had waited for us exactly where we had left him earlier that day when the Russians forced us out of the truck. He drove us to a point where the Danube separated the American and Russian zones in Austria. From there he led us through deep grass on the riverbank to a small boat waiting to ferry us across, two at a time. The boat left at intervals between the passing Russian border patrols. Miraculously, we all made it. After everyone had reached the far bank, we exulted to be free from the Russians at last and safe in the American zone.

After we arrived in Linz, personnel from the Jewish refugee organization met us, checked our identities, and drove us to a tent inside a refugee camp there. They planned for us to depart Linz in a few days, first for Italy and then by boat to Palestine. Once in Palestine, we were to join Jewish forces fighting the Arabs. Of course, their plan conflicted with ours, since Gabriel and I were headed for Salzburg. While in Linz, we found a driver willing to take us there. Even this transportation service, however, did not get us to our ultimate destination. Once in Salzburg, we still needed to cross yet another border, this time from Austria into Germany.

After arriving in Salzburg, Gabriel and I found and hired yet another guide, one who had a plan to get us across the Austrian border and into Germany. He would take us south by train along the Austrian border to a station stop near the Alps, where we would proceed by foot over the Alps into Germany. We boarded the train in Salzburg together with a third refugee, a young cello player who carried his large instrument with him. We got off at the designated Austrian station in the Alpine foothills, crossed a small bridge, and started climbing in darkness.

Our route over the Alps required that we pass through the mountains near Berchtesgaden of all places—Hitler's wartime retreat. My mind wrestled with the troubling realization that not far from us Hitler had vacationed while the SS carried out his ghastly extermination orders, orders that doomed my parents and millions of other innocent people and nearly did in Gabriel and me. Passing by Hitler's lair, the irony did not escape me that I was alive with a promising future in America and he was dead with a bullet in his head—rough but deserved justice for his heinous crimes. Climbing the Alps in dense clouds and utter darkness, we lost contact with the straggling cello player, who could not maintain our pace during the steep climb. Nearing the German border at the misty mountaintop, we paid a well-earned fee to our guide. He waved, said "Auf wiedersehen," and left. Gabriel and I entered Germany on our own, still frightened yet confident that soon we would be free.

Descending the mountain road, we entered Berchtesgaden at first light and heard the distant sound of American voices. We never saw anyone, however, just blinking lights among the thick stand of fir trees. The presence of American soldiers both heartened and frightened us. Yes, we had arrived in Germany, but we had no papers, and we still had a long trip ahead before reaching Munich. Treading cautiously downhill, we eventually found the railroad station at daybreak. We used our rudimentary German to buy tickets to Munich—the true beginning of our genuine freedom. Awaiting the train to Munich, we tried to hide our muddy shoes under the station-room bench. We wanted to avoid suspicion by local travelers that we had entered Germany illegally.

We boarded the train with other passengers and eventually arrived in Munich. We took a streetcar headed toward Moelh Strasse, the location of the Jewish refugee agency. The streetcar conductor, however, forgot to tell us when we had reached our destination. Consequently, we circled Munich again before finally reaching the stop near the agency.

At the agency, we found a sympathetic man with a jeep at his disposal. He kindly drove us to the Neu Freimann displaced person camp on the outskirts of Munich. The DP camp was a former housing project for German working families, but now it was occupied solely by refugees and guarded by unarmed Jewish police. The camp administrators assigned us a small top-floor room with two beds in a two-story, single-family house. They also gave us IDs as well as ration cards that entitled us to goods from US volunteer organizations, like the Joint Distribution Committee. The ration cards gave us free access to Spam, toothpaste, toothbrushes, soap, bread, and lots of toilet paper. In my entire previous life I had never used anything but printed paper in the bathroom!

At the camp, I joined the local police department and was assigned to guard against cigarette smugglers entering the camp. I had no legal authority, however, to act in the event of a problem. Jews ran the department (all the American forces remained in central Munich). Over many nights I stood four-hour watches, stationed on the camp's periphery or at its main gate. Despite my conscientious guard duty, the enormous cigarette smuggling business in Bavaria, especially in US cigarettes, continued to thrive. Nevertheless, I had made a dramatic transition over the past three years—from a Nazi concentration-camp prisoner under constant guard to a DP camp policeman guarding others.

Among the Jewish leaders in the Neu Freimann camp were rabbis, who urged everyone to go to Palestine to fight for the Jewish state. When one particular rabbi pressed me to join up, I replied, "Why don't you go?" His answer, "Someone must stay behind in Germany to do the recruiting," did not impress me. Instead, I stuck to Uncle David's advice and waited for berthing space to open on a navy ship bound for the United States. Gabriel and I already had paid a high price for being Jewish, and we were entitled to recover our lives in America.

My lot continued to improve during my wait in Munich, as I started searching for a paying job. I discovered a man who came from Szamosujvar, Transylvania, where my Frenkel grandparents had lived and I had attended gymnasium. He ran the main dining room for the Joint Distribution Committee located on Moelh Strasse, and he needed someone to run a secondary dining room for staff workers. Despite my youth, temporary status, and inexperience, I decided to apply, and he hired me on the spot. He trusted me, even though he knew that I was just waiting for my ship to America.

The dining-room job was excellent, and it placed me in lively central Munich. I befriended Fritz Jahleh, the German cook, and his pretty wife, who served in the main dining room. She introduced me to her sister, and the four of us took motorcycle tours around scenic Chiemsee and Tegernsee. I lived on Moelh Strasse in a clean rented apartment and owned several changes of clothing, a motorcycle, and a small hand-camera. I had a few German marks in my pocket, a good job in the dining room, plenty to eat, and a new lease on life. Indeed, I was sufficiently well-off to provide modest financial help to Gabriel, who was attending university in Munich. One day Uncle Max made a surprising appearance in Munich with his new wife, Margot, and sons Eddie and Nathan. Max's first wife, Sidona, had died after we left Romania. Despite the unexpected arrival of family, however, I felt deep down a lingering sense of profound loss. My parents were gone forever, as was the rest of my Transylvanian family, including my grandparents, uncles, and aunts, as well as my other Hungarian relatives living outside of Budapest.

After about a year in Munich, my number came up on the wait list. I had to report to the port of Bremerhaven on a specific date in September 1949. There I would embark for America aboard a US Navy ship, the USS *General JHM Rae*. The US government paid for my trip under a special immigration quota for 50,000 DPs from the American zone in Germany. Gabriel, however, did not join me in the voyage. While attending university, he had met and married a German girl and decided to remain behind in Munich. Consequently, at age twenty, I ended my stimulating year in Munich and embarked alone on another journey, this time headed for a new life in the New World.

10.
A New Beginning

On the evening of September 5, 1949, after an uneventful crossing, the USS *General JHM Rae* sailed into New York Bay and dropped anchor. I spent the entire night gazing at the bouncing headlights of Brooklyn traffic and contemplating the promise of America. The next morning the ship weighed anchor, sailed past the Statue of Liberty, entered the Hudson River, and eased up to the 34th Street pier at the Port of New York. At age twenty, with a ten-dollar bill in my pocket and all my worldly possessions in a small briefcase, I descended the gangplank to the pier and went through US Customs. Finally in America, I eagerly awaited the long-anticipated reunion with my remaining family.

Uncle David Ince, my mother's oldest brother, met me on arrival and escorted me to his Pontiac convertible parked nearby. As we drove east on 34th Street before turning north toward the 59th Street Bridge, Uncle David pointed out the Empire State Building, which I had already recognized. I could only think how lucky I was! We headed through Queens to Long Island and eventually arrived at his new waterfront home on Ballantine Lane at Kings Point in Great Neck, Long Island. His two younger brothers, Uncles Eugene and Ernest, were waiting for us.

Uncle David was a reasonably well-off medical-insurance agent with a degree in law from Europe. Uncles Eugene and Ernest were hairdressers, both financially comfortable but apparently envious of David's greater financial success. I soon discovered that Ernest and Eugene had not been on speaking terms with David and had not seen him for many years. Thus, my arrival had precipitated an uncomfortable, and probably undesired, reunion of the three brothers at David's Kings Point house. The uncles asked a few perfunctory questions about my travails, and in return I asked what they had done during the war. David's wife, Helen, interjected that they had anxiously searched the survivor lists for David's relatives, implying that their search had engendered as much suffering as I had endured in the camps. Her concern for the fate of my family seemed casual, insufficient, and belated. It provided the first disturbing evidence of my relatives' wartime indifference to our mortal peril. The thought upsets and grieves me to this day.

In the course of our meeting, my three uncles huddled together, speaking to one another alternately in Hungarian and English. They were exchanging views on how much each was willing to contribute toward my support, and for how long. Since I spoke no English at the time, I missed much of the detailed wrangling. Finally, David summarized their decision for me in Hungarian. Collectively they would give me a certain amount each month to live on and to finance my training as a hairdresser. A hairdresser! Without inquiring about or considering my background, interests, or talents, they summarily decreed that I should become a hairdresser. Furthermore, throughout his summation, Uncle David emphasized that the sooner I became self-sufficient the better.

This initial encounter with my three American uncles was both uncomfortable and disheartening. They made no serious inquiry into my camp experience and showed no empathy for my suffering and loss. They never once mentioned their two lost sisters—my mother, Ida, and my aunt Magda—or their lost half-brother, my uncle Erwin. I came to the United States expecting to be embraced by my few remaining relatives. Instead, they ignored my feelings altogether and dwelled almost entirely on money. Money was the farthest thing from my mind. I was looking for familial compassion, loving support, and personal encouragement. I thought I deserved it from these close remaining relatives. But they offered none.

When Gabriel arrived in the United States about a month later, their greeting of him was even colder. By the time of his arrival, Gabriel had divorced his German wife. These relatives expressed their disapproval of his divorce by refusing him any financial assistance. They left Gabriel entirely on his own, providing him neither material nor emotional support. Consequently, Gabriel initially supported himself doing manual labor on assembly lines while attending night school. In 1956, he earned a BSc degree at Cooper Union and then earned an MS degree at City College. Some twenty years later, Georgetown University awarded Gabriel a PhD in mathematics. He spent the balance of his distinguished career as a scientist at the Defense Advanced Research Projects Agency (DARPA). Gabriel eventually remarried. He and his wife, Naomi, have a son, David, and a daughter, Debbie, and now live in Pittsburgh.

This initial treatment by our American relatives increased my sense of loss and left me feeling totally on my own. About ten days later, I left David's home and moved to Philadelphia, where Uncle Ernest owned a beauty shop in the Benjamin Franklin Hotel. I lived in an apartment on Clinton Street with my cousin Danny Weitzner. Danny was the son of Aunt Nelli, my mother's sister, who had died several years before my arrival in America. During my time in Philadelphia, Uncle Ernest's wife, Helen, became a confidante—the only family member who provided me with any emotional support during this difficult period of adjustment. I enrolled in a hairdresser-training course and also attended classes on spoken English. I needed to communicate in my adopted country, so the language course on the 1,000 most commonly used words in English seemed a quick route to minimal fluency. After completing training, I launched my brief hairdressing career at Charles of the Ritz Beauty Salon at the Wannamaker Department Store in downtown Philadelphia.

My youth and thick Hungarian accent drew a steady and generous female clientele, but shampooing, combing, and cutting women's hair was definitely not my calling. Increasingly drawn to agricultural interests from my rural Transylvanian roots, I decided to complete my education in agriculture begun after the war in Tirgu Mures. I took an entrance exam at Temple University, but the admissions office advised that I needed additional US schooling. I had to supplement my Romanian high-school education and become proficient in English before the university would consider my application. So I gave up on Temple and decided to look elsewhere.

In 1951, I telephoned the Delaware Valley College of Science and Agriculture (DVC) in Doylestown, Pennsylvania, and spoke to Dean Donald Meyer. He encouraged me to visit DVC. Although it is now nondenominational, DVC was founded in 1898 by Rabbi Krauskopf to support the Zionist movement by training Jewish boys who volunteered to work on farms in Palestine. Outfitted in a new blue-and-white seersucker suit, I boarded the train for Doylestown to meet with Dean Meyer. During our initial interview, he accepted my application. Furthermore, after learning that my total assets amounted to $500 saved from work as a hairdresser, he awarded me a work-related scholarship. DVC paid me sixty cents per hour toward my room and board in exchange for performing various on-campus jobs—sorting and stacking books in the library, waiting on tables, canning fruits and vegetables, and cleaning the cow barn, among others. I worked these jobs with another recent immigrant, Josh Feldstein, who later became DVC president.

Shortly after moving to the DVC campus, I received a letter from my former landlady on Clinton Street in Philadelphia. Her letter stated that she owned two residential buildings on Clinton Street and wanted to appoint me as her heir since she had no living relatives. I thought then that money had no real value and that all I truly needed was close and caring relatives. I never replied to her offer, a failure that I later regretted. I have since reflected on how that fortuitous legacy might have financed my later business ventures.

Following my first year at DVC, I changed my initial major from agriculture to the food industry, which offered a broader scientific grounding and greater financial prospects. Whereas basic agricultural training was useful in rural Romania, I believed that a more scientifically oriented education was necessary for success in America. This realization came to me after observing the different job levels at the Campbell Soup factory in Camden, New Jersey, where I worked that first summer. In 1955, I graduated from DVC with a BSc in food industry. No family member saw fit to attend the graduation ceremony. This saddened me. It reminded me yet again that my family was gone and I was on my own.

My first position was with United Dairy Equipment, a New Jersey company that installed and managed offshore dairy-processing plants. United Dairy hired me as technical supervisor for six milk plants located on US Air Force and Navy bases in Bermuda, Canada, and Greenland. My job was to assure that the six plants produced healthy dairy products and complied with military contract specifications and FDA food-safety standards. Since my technical knowledge of FDA food-safety regulations surpassed that of the medical doctors overseeing the plants, I felt immediate confidence in my job skills.

I lived primarily in the BOQ (Bachelor Officer Quarters) at the US Air Force Base in St. John's, Newfoundland, but traveled frequently among all six plants to assure that they produced quality, FDA-compliant products. I was constantly on the move, flying on military aircraft, eating in local officers' mess halls, and sleeping in BOQs on site. Business travel took me to Bermuda; Goose Bay, Labrador; Thule, Sondrestrom, and Narsarssuak, Greenland; and Harmon Air Force Base at Stephenville and the navy base at Argentia, Newfoundland. Compensating for the cold weather and incessant travel was the natural wonder of Greenland. I had read about it as a child—the glaciers and ice caps, the long durations of darkness and daylight, and the glorious aurora borealis.

Following eighteen months of overseas work as a tax-exempt foreign resident, I declined my employer's offer of a promotion to senior company representative. Instead, I returned to New York City with my savings, intent on furthering my education. I took night classes toward a master's degree in biology at New York University with the idea of eventually becoming a medical doctor like my father. I paid for school by working as a laboratory technician in the pathology departments of various hospitals (Bellevue and NYU). It took me over four years, until 1960, to complete the course requirements. When it came time for me to write a master's thesis, however, I had reached the decision to opt out of a career in medicine and return to one in business. Shortly thereafter, I accepted a job offer as manager of Borden's milk-processing plant in St. Thomas, US Virgin Islands.

The Borden job provided not only a pleasant tropical climate but also a relaxing change from the frigid northern latitudes and constant air travel with United Dairy and from the daily stress of New York City life. In St. Thomas, I drove a green two-seater MG convertible and co-owned an eighteen-foot day-sailer with my friend David Lord (a psychologist originally from Vermont). We often sailed together among the Caribbean islands (St. Thomas, St. John, St. Croix, and Tortola) and enjoyed the marvelous beaches at Bluebeard's Castle on St. Thomas and Caneel Bay on St. John. After two years on St. Thomas, however, I began to feel restless and tired of the tourists. I needed to move on to another challenge.

In 1962, I received a telegram through the governor's office on St. Thomas from a contracting officer at the US Air Force base in Frankfurt, Germany. He was responding to my request to be placed on their competitive bidders' list for dairy plants at overseas military bases. His telegram was a Request for Proposal (RFP), soliciting my bid on a five-year contract to build and operate a dairy-processing plant at the air force base in Peshawar, Pakistan. Jumping at the opportunity, I flew to Germany, submitted a bid, and landed the contract. I lacked capital to finance the project, however, so I quickly acquired two silent partners in New York City. One partner was my cousin Danny, who by then was a practicing psychiatrist, and the other was his neighbor in the wholesale textile business. In addition, Uncle David and Aunt Helen loaned me $30,000, a debt they later forgave. I quit my job in St. Thomas, moved back to New York, and opened a small business office at 180 Madison Avenue near 34th Street. After successfully installing, staffing, and operating the Peshawar plant, I received additional opportunities with the military, and my international business grew.

In September 1967, friends of my cousin Danny and his wife, Tilly, introduced me to Rita Maduro, a sweet, educated, and cultured artist. Rita had graduated from Skidmore College and was living and working in New York. She was born in Panama, descended from Sephardic Jews who traced their family lineage back hundreds of years to the Spanish Inquisition. Initially a little wary of my Hungarian accent, Rita declined my dinner invitation. Instead, she suggested we go out for drinks. The lounge that we visited on East 74th Street in Manhattan had few customers but loud music, which interfered with our conversation. When I asked the bartender to lower the music, Rita thought it commendable that a lone customer would make such a bold request of a New York establishment.

On our second date, Rita joined me on a ride to DVC in Doylestown. I wanted to inquire whether DVC could recommend someone to manage the Pakistan milk plant. During our four-and-a-half-hour round trip, Rita and I discovered and discussed at length our mutual love of opera. At the end of our trip we stopped by Danny and Tilly's house, where I played with their three children. This too impressed Rita, and we continued dating for a year. On November 2, 1968, Rita and I were married in Temple Emanuel in New York, with a reception following at the Regency Hotel on Park Avenue. All my relatives attended this event. Rita's father, Fred, gave her away to me that day with the following admonition: "Take good care of my daughter." I have honored his wish. The following year we moved from New York City to New Preston, Connecticut, located above beautiful Lake Waramaug in the northwestern part of the state. There we raised our two children, Victoria and Nicholas, and have remained ever since.

By 1968, as the result of my initial business ventures, I acquired sufficient funds to establish my own company without any partners, Servrite International, Ltd. The air force awarded Servrite contracts to build plants in Goose Bay, Labrador; Ankara and Adana, Turkey; and Athens, Greece. In addition, the navy awarded Servrite contracts to install plants on the US Navy bases at Kenitra, Morocco; Rota, Spain; Guantánamo Bay, Cuba; and Naples, Italy. Then came Servrite's largest contracts, with the US Air Force in Yokohama and Okinawa, Japan. Producing every dairy product typically found in US supermarkets, Servrite's dairy-processing plants supplied army, navy, and air force land and sea units from the Caribbean to the Mediterranean to the Pacific.

Over four decades, I performed military contract work under the Servrite banner without any outside financial support. Throughout Servrite's long history, I averaged approximately twenty years at each dairy plant that I operated for the US military—unprecedented contractual longevity that sustained my business. Furthermore, I managed all these international contracts from an administrative office near my home in the Connecticut countryside. The tradeoff for the pastoral setting of my business office was my frequent intercontinental travel. I remained a globetrotter.

The key to my growing business, my longevity with each military contract, and my overall business success was threefold: my technical savvy; my ability to perform fast, detailed, and accurate calculations; and my investment of $15,000 in an IBM Model 5100 portable computer. I bought the computer in the early 1970s, long before its value had become apparent to my major business competitors. The computer enabled me to perform cost and pricing calculations quickly and accurately for the large number of container sizes and product ingredients needed for the many different product types specified in my military contracts.

While my competitors required several weeks for six full-time administrative staff members using adding machines to prepare bid calculations on military contracts, I prepared my bids in a matter of days with only two staff members. Similarly, my cost was lower than my competitors' for calculating the quarterly price adjustments required by contract. My lower overhead costs (by two-thirds) and my shorter response time (hours versus days) enabled me regularly to underbid large competitors with thousands of employees. Consequently, for many years I was operating on average six plants, while all of my competitors fought over the one remaining contract.

My business, however, was not all smooth sailing. After four years of operations, Servrite faced a serious challenge. From 1972 to 1974, I operated a milk plant for the navy at San Giorgio a Cremano, a town between Naples and Pompeii, just as the Italian lira strengthened against the dollar and adversely affected our revenue. My navy contract provided price adjustments for fluctuations in the cost of various raw materials but did not provide sufficient adjustment for other costs, like rent and labor, that I paid in lira. As our local costs in lira escalated with the dollar's precipitous decline in relative value, I urgently needed an adjustment in contract terms for Servrite to continue supplying dairy products to the Sixth Fleet in the Mediterranean.

My instinct for survival prompted me to seek advice from the navy, which recommended that I contact the Washington, DC, law firm of Sellers, Conner & Cuneo. The firm assigned my case to Chuck O'Connor, who successfully argued for extraordinary contractual relief under Public Law 85-804. The resultant $700,000 award allowed me to break even on the Naples contract and to continue Servrite's otherwise successful business operations. Chuck and I have remained close friends ever since, and he continues to be my valued counselor.

On May 2, 2009, DVC honored me with its Distinguished Service Award from the Food Science Hall of Fame. I appreciated this recognition for my long business career in the dairy field. DVC taught me well about the demanding US federal food-processing standards that my business needed to meet. I consistently satisfied these standards in all my many business operations, not only overseas military contracts but also commercial contracts, including one in Panama under the NEVADA Brand.

The operational freedom and financial security afforded by my business career had enormous psychological value. After the terrible insecurity caused by my yearlong captivity as a teenager in the Nazi concentration camps, the United States provided me with a newfound freedom and a unique business opportunity. I was able to secure my financial future, provide for my family, and educate my two children, Victoria and Nicholas. The psychological relief was enormous. Indeed, my long business relationship with the US Navy—especially in Rota, Spain—represented, for me, the best of America. It involved the mutual trust and respect that I associated with my early Boy Scout experience in Hadad and the national ideals and values that I admired when becoming an American citizen in 1954.

I have more than reclaimed my life from the Nazis, and as I look back over the past eight decades, I have much to be grateful for. At the same time, I have an abiding sadness that Rita and I were unable to share our fulfilling life with my parents, grandparents, uncle, and aunt who were killed by the Nazis. They no doubt would be as proud as we are of our children, our grandchildren, and our life in America. Victoria (Tori) earned her BA from Wheaton College and her master's degree in education from Lesley College. Tori specializes in teaching learning-disabled children. She and her husband, Tom, have two boys, Theo and Simon. Nicholas (Nick) earned his BA at Skidmore College. Nick is a talent manager in the entertainment business. He and his wife, Nanci, have two sons, Oliver and Logan. Reflecting on my wonderful marriage and family and on my successful business career, I am conscious of having realized the dual American dream of personal fulfillment and material success.

In the 1990s, I learned the fate of my family from the World War II archives in Arolsen, Germany. The Arolsen files disclosed that my father was murdered at Auschwitz in 1945, soon after his separation from Gabriel and me at Buchenwald; that my mother, Ida, grandparents Morton and Cili, and aunt Magda also were murdered at Auschwitz in June 1944, immediately upon arrival there; and that Uncle Ervin was spared immediate death at Auschwitz only to be shipped to another camp where he met the same fate. Having tragically lost the love and support of my own parents and relatives as a teenager, I have valued my own family all the more and have considered every moment of family life precious.

11.
Trying to Recover the Past

In April 1981, for the first time since my surreptitious departure in 1948, I returned to Romania on my own to revisit the scenes of my youth. I flew to Bucharest and then to Cluj (Kolozsvar), drove to Hodod (Hadad), and later returned to Bucharest via Gherla (Szamosujvar). After arriving at Bucharest airport, I went to claim my bags on the conveyor belt and found a Romanian customs agent waiting next to them. Standing there silently, he looked alternately at me and my bags. Without asking me to open my bags or waving me on, he clearly intended to bar my entry—until I pulled out a carton of cigarettes and handed him four packs. Without a moment's hesitation, he took the cigarette packs and waved me through. Obviously, nothing much had changed in Romania over the thirty-three years since I had left. Bribes still fueled its economy.

On the taxi ride into Bucharest city center, I could see that the streets, buildings, and city sites looked very much as they were, including the movie house and the department store built in 1945. There was no new construction, traffic remained characteristically hectic, and the old trolley still ran downtown to the Royal Palace, where police shot at demonstrators after the war. No. 9 Dr. Victor Polony Street, where Gabriel and I shared a top floor room and received Uncle David's phone call inviting us to America, were unchanged. The Intercontinental Hotel where I was staying was new, and the shooting and demonstrations had stopped, but everything else appeared just the same as I had left it, although considerably more rundown. The vibrant capital city of my post-liberation seemed drab and drained of energy, and the people had recovered little of their former spirit under the repressive rule of Nikolai Ceausescu.

Since my two Frenkel uncles had left Bucharest years before, I had no reason to stay there more than a day, so I flew to Cluj. The airport was the city's one significant postwar innovation, but otherwise, Cluj presented the same colorless picture as Bucharest. The house on Matthias Square where I lived with my mother in 1943, the butcher shop next door, the local bookstore, my middle school, and the neighborhood drugstore were just as I last saw them. So too were my mother's school, the Marianum; my grandfather Frenkel's house; the synagogue with its decorative round balls protruding from the rooftop; and the hospital where I was born. One thing, however, was noticeably different. None of the Jewish people whom I had known in Cluj, nor any of their descendants, were there.

I have since learned that some knowledgeable Jewish residents of Cluj avoided Auschwitz by buying safe passage into Switzerland from Adolf Eichmann. They never shared with their Jewish Hungarian brethren their insider information about the Nazi genocide or about the necessity and means to escape their imminent danger. Consequently, other Jewish families in the Cluj area, like ours, never understood their dire peril or their potential remedy. On several occasions in New York City I met one such Jewish family from Cluj. They never explained their actions or apologized either for obtaining special treatment from the Nazis or for not alerting the rest of the local Jewish community.

I retraced the paths that I walked so often with my mother—over the Samos River Bridge to the city park, into the English garden with its lake and swans, and on to the roadside benches in front of the church and the statue of mounted King Matthias. Remembering these experiences with Mother, I was overcome with sadness. Then sadness gradually transitioned to anger, as I pondered the Nazi murder of my entire family and my Jewish friends and neighbors—all killed wantonly, without justification. My April 29, 1981, letter home to Rita, Tori, and Nick captured my outrage over "what they did to all our people … because we are Jewish." Romania was clearly the poorer for it.

I arrived by car in Hodod. Except for the new steel electricity poles that lined the main street, Hodod had changed for the worse. The farmland was barren, the courtyard of the Banfi estate was empty, and the Jews and their synagogue were missing. The Jewish cemetery was overgrown with weeds that hid the individual headstones of people I knew and whom Father had treated.

I located the house of my old friend and mentor, Uncle Mihaly. He had moved from his former house below the Banfi estate to another house on the main road near the flour mill. Uncle Mihaly had lost weight, his hearing was going, and he appeared depressed. Instead of the warm and engaging personality that I remembered so fondly, Mihaly was emotionless. He perked up slightly when he let me pat his favorite horse, tied up in a small shed opposite his kitchen, and then he recounted his sad story. For his many years of faithful service to Count Banfi, the Communist government of Romania (1947–1989) had sentenced Mihaly to thirty years in a Russian gulag. He labored all those years in a forest coal mine. As a consequence, he developed a debilitating respiratory condition, emphysema. The gulag had drained the life out of him—all because he performed a menial job for a Hungarian count.

Uncle Mihaly and his wife were trying to rebuild their life in Hodod, struggling to survive on the produce of their small garden and on their few pigs and goats, without any outside source of income. As I entered his house, one of his grown children offered me a chair, where I sat reminiscing with Mihaly at the kitchen table. During our conversation he told me that Moses Adorjan was living in Gherla, and I resolved to visit him there. Mihaly was most grateful for the few things I brought him—cigarettes, cheeses, candy, and other food items, purchased from the air force PX near my milk plant in Athens, Greece. Then he took me outside to view some of the familiar sights of my childhood.

His home was near a hothouse for drying prunes, located just across the road from the Banfi cattle yard. As a child I watched his bulls siring there. Just two hundred feet away was the flour mill and beyond it the Banfi estate. But I was left to imagine what the vast estate had been like in my youth, since nothing much was happening there. The estate was idle, its vibrant agricultural community gone. We walked straight through the castle courtyard to the castle door, since I could not bear to stop and visit our second home in the courtyard. The painful memory of loss overcame me. I had to keep moving.

As we reach the castle entrance, Mihaly hesitated and refused to enter the castle with me. Standing before me in the light pants and T-shirt covering his thin frame, Mihaly registered only pain. The Romanian caretakers at the castle had badly mistreated him, and he wanted nothing more to do with them. Approaching the castle, I noticed that the two pine trees that had flanked the front door were cut down. I entered the castle and wandered alone through its barren rooms. The furniture was gone— looted by the peasants and Communists. A listless crew of three low-ranking officials sat in one of the castle's many empty rooms, presumably there to prevent further looting or destruction of the Banfi property. At the time of my visit, Hodod had more Romanians than Hungarians living there, since the Romanian government had subsidized the transfer of Romanians from other provinces in order to achieve a majority Romanian population in northern Transylvania.

No one farmed the Banfi estate, no cattle stood in the courtyard barns, and no trees bore fruits or walnuts. Indeed, there were no trees; they were all cut down to supply wood for Soviet Russia. Hodod was rundown, and most of the people I had known were gone. Not a single Jew had returned to reside there after the war. As I walked back out of the castle toward Uncle Mihaly, I became consumed by the same sense of estrangement I had felt during my postwar visit to Hodod in 1945. At that time, apart from Uncle Mihaly, Moses, the pharmacist, and the standoffish Richters, only one local citizen recognized me and remembered my father.

This visit I did meet one other childhood friend, Gyuri Kulcsar, who lived two houses away from our last home on the main street. I had dinner at his home, located where our landlord's tavern previously stood just across the courtyard from our last home. At the end of the evening, as I started to leave, Gyuri handed me a wooden spigot that he made for his wine barrels, a reminder of our surreptitious drinking escapades as youngsters in the Banfi wine cellar. Other than Gyuri and Mihaly's family, none of my childhood friends remained in Hodod. Bidding farewell to these few remaining friends, I headed south to Gherla hoping to reunite with my old friend and mentor, Moses Adorjan.

On Gherla's main street I stopped at a business directly across from my grandmother Cili's old textile store to inquire of its Jewish owner about Gherla's current Jewish population. He told me that few Jews now lived in Gherla, perhaps a dozen. Before the war, this was a city with a thriving Jewish population numbering in the hundreds. Most of those lucky enough to have survived the Nazis decided to move to Israel. While I was in Gherla, I saw none of its few remaining Jews. I drove to see the house that Father had purchased in the early 1940s for Aunt Magda, Uncle Erwin, Gabriel, and me when I was in school there. (In 1948, Gabriel and I had permitted Uncle Feri to sell the house and keep the proceeds in gratitude for his generosity toward us.) Then I drove around the city—by my grandparents' house where grandfather Frenkel had his tailor shop, the Armenian church where I sang in the choir, and the old synagogue where the family attended services—to take pictures.

I eventually found Moses, who was living across the street from my old gymnasium. After my initial joy at his warm greeting, I was soon overcome with sadness. Walking into the kitchen, I saw his wife by the stove, and I was shocked at how old she looked, mostly bald with a few wisps of gray hair. I remembered her as the most beautiful girl in Hadad. Newspapers covered the floor of their modest two-room apartment to protect their simple carpets. They had barely enough to eat. Their downtrodden appearance spoke volumes about their life under the Romanian Communists, which Moses recounted during my visit.

In early 1945, as the Russians were approaching Hodod and the Romanians were reasserting control of northern Transylvania, Count Banfi asked Moses to transport the count's valuables into Hungary. The count's charge was Moses's undoing. Shortly after the war, the newly installed Communist government under Gheorghe Gheorghiu-Dej (1947–65) prosecuted Moses for allegedly stealing the count's property and sent him to jail. Presumably the government thought that Moses would return or at least identify the location of the Banfi wealth rather than face imprisonment. Moses, of course, had taken nothing and, thus, had nothing to disclose. Postwar Romania was clearly no place for Hungarians like Moses and Mihaly. As my train began to pull away from Gherla station, Moses stood on the platform, and we stared at one another through my open train window. His parting words were sad and prophetic: "We probably will not see each other again."

During my visit to Romania in 1981, Nikolai Ceausescu was in power (1965–89) and Romania had suffered for it. Steam locomotives still pulled the trains, towns like Hodod still had no automobiles, and food remained scarce, despite Romania's vast fertile farmlands. According to my Hodod friend, Gyuri, the Soviet Union forced the Ceausescu government to export most of its agricultural produce to Russia, which made it unavailable to feed the Romanian people. With the Communist takeover of Romania in 1947, capitalists and entrepreneurs like my uncles Max and Feri saw the handwriting on the wall and left. One midnight in 1948, Max and his young family stole across the Hungarian border. To avoid detection, Max never even told his older, married daughter Judith about his plans to emigrate from Romania to Israel. Uncle Feri followed soon thereafter. After several years in Israel, both Max and Feri finally settled in the United States.

My second "visit" to Romania was entirely imaginary. It was a psychic journey in 1984, as I lay helplessly bedridden for three weeks at home in Connecticut. This was the worst possible time to be incapacitated. The US Air Force had just awarded me one of my largest five-year military contracts, in Okinawa, Japan. Lifting a tire for Servrite's newly acquired refrigeration truck, I had seriously strained my back and could not move. Confined to bed in New Preston, I began to reminisce. The memories overwhelmed and depressed me. Suddenly I had lost my mobility and self-sufficiency, and this helplessness brought to mind my childhood captivity in the Nazi camps. This memory in turn led to excessive anxiety about my business and my ability to support my family. Then I began to recall my father's constant financial worries, my lost identity in the camps, and my family's murder there. This dark past haunted my entire convalescence in 1984, as it does even now whenever my thoughts drift back to the past.

In the summer of 1987, when Tori was seventeen and Nick fourteen, I decided it was time to show them my roots. This time I actually did return to Romania, the second visit since my postwar emigration. Rita and I flew with the children to Frankfurt, Germany, purchased a Saab, and drove to Munich. From Munich we retraced my steps of 1948, to Salzburg and Vienna, Austria; Budapest, Hungary; and finally Romania. We stayed overnight in Chiemsee outside of Munich, where Rita photographed me leaning on the sculpture of the reclining goddess in front of mad King Ludwig's Castle. In 1949, I had posed at the same spot during a visit with my German friends, the Jahlehs, who worked with me at the Munich restaurant. We proceeded east through Salzburg to Vienna before making our way into Hungary.

Although subject to a Communist government at the time, Hungary was genuinely pleasant. We stayed at a hotel near Lake Balaton, Hungary's largest lake, and we enjoyed many fine restaurants. Whenever we heard

Gypsy violin music, however, I invariably broke into tears—they were playing songs my mother would sing to us as children. Traveling on to Budapest, we walked the Vaci Utca, the city's main shopping center; took a cruise on the Danube; and visited the main synagogue.

Budapest's Forum Hotel, on the Pest side of the city where we stayed, is near the Chain Bridge (Lance Hid), which was bombed and partly submerged in the Danube at the war's end. In 1945, I had waded through the river on the submerged bridge to reach my relatives in Buda. The next day, we drove to the Romanian border near Oradea. The Romanian border guard asked Nick, just a young teenager at the time, if he was carrying any firearms—a preposterous concern and an obvious shakedown for bribes. The guard did not lift the gate until I offered him four packs of cigarettes. These shakedowns still were the norm in Communist Romania.

At each location we visited in Romania, we could stay only in the government-designated hotel. In Oradea, our hotel had a grand dining room with tall ceilings, numerous tables, and a large menu. It had few customers, however, and offered only four choices from the menu. Slim pickings indeed. No one in the hotel smiled and no one answered me in Hungarian—even though the staff was mostly Hungarian—because Ceausescu barred the use of any spoken Hungarian.

We called upon my childhood friend Joska Richter, who lived near the Romanian border in a rural suburb of Oradea with his wife and two older children. Joska owned one-half acre of land and a small house with a separate kitchen, outhouse, and vegetable garden. He fed his family from his garden produce and made his own wine clandestinely. Joska invited us to dinner in their otherwise unused dining room with its newspaper-covered floor.

From Oradea, we drove to Cluj to visit my cousin Judith (Max's daughter). Judith married in 1946 and had two boys. In consideration of her young family, Judith decided to remain in Romania after the war, even after her father left for Israel. Because Judith's husband was a businessman before the war, the new Communist government denied him the opportunity to work. Consequently, Judith had to become the family breadwinner, as a bookkeeper in an agricultural business and later in a bookstore.

After the war, the Romanian government initially accepted Jews. But after the so-called doctors' plot in the Soviet Union (1952–53), Jews fell out of favor with Stalin and his satellite governments like Romania. (In December 1952, Stalin fabricated charges that prominent Jewish doctors in Moscow had planned to assassinate Soviet leaders. This false allegation led to show trials, massive anti-Semitic propaganda, job dismissals, and false arrests that resulted in Jewish executions or imprisonments in the gulags.)

Judith whispered to us that she intended to emigrate from Romania to Israel. Even in her own home, she feared that her neighbors might overhear and report her conversations. Indeed, she worried that her apartment was bugged by government agents who might thwart her plans. (In 1990, Judith successfully emigrated to Israel to join her two sons, and has lived there ever since.) Although Judith had sufficient room for all of us, we had to stay in the hotel prescribed by the government. Romanian law prohibited Romanian citizens from offering accommodations to anyone but immediate family, a criterion we did not meet. The Romanian government obviously intended to promote local business and also to keep close tabs on all foreigners.

For generations prior to World War II, Cluj was the cultural center of northern Transylvania. In 1987, however, this ancient Hungarian city looked rundown, even though it still maintained an opera house and a medical school. Our assigned hotel was comfortable, but its meals were nearly inedible. Obviously Cluj was suffering the same food shortage as other Romanian cities. Judith's housekeeper, however, lived in the countryside and had her own garden. When she came to clean the house, she regularly brought Judith fresh vegetables, and consequently, we took most of our meals in Cluj with Judith.

From Cluj we headed north on a two-and-a-half-hour ride to Hodod with a picnic lunch packed by Judith, since we would find no food available anywhere along the way. Dotting the Transylvanian countryside along our route, we saw peasants laboring in the fields, still working without the benefit of heavy machinery. Rita likened the passing scene to a Bruegel painting of farmers with pitchforks and shovels. We approached Hodod via Cehu Silvaniei, the nearby town with the train station. From this station, the Hungarian fascists had shipped Hadad's Jewish population by train to Satu Mare and then to Auschwitz in May 1944. Nearing Hodod, we passed a horse-drawn carriage—a classic scene from my childhood. (See photograph.)

Hodod showed no evidence of progress since my last visit in 1981. We called upon Uncle Mihaly, who was warm and gracious to Rita, the children, and me. His appearance surprised them, however—his two-day stubble, missing teeth, and bent posture. He welcomed us into his dark, primitive house, where his aging wife stood by the kitchen stove in her black robe. Newspapers covered the mud floor and flies buzzed everywhere. He offered to slaughter one of his goats to feed us dinner, but we declined his generosity. From Hodod we headed south to Gherla, where I drove past those places that factored so prominently in my youth. Summoning up remembrances of my past, however, gradually darkened my mood, and the family eventually insisted that we move on to our next destination, Belgrade, Yugoslavia.

At the Yugoslav border, we again encountered acquisitive Romanian border guards. We waited while they checked the automobile in front of us, ostensibly looking for illicit goods. The two female motorists hardly seemed like smugglers, so the guards most likely were angling for a bribe. I came prepared for the shakedown with cartons of cigarettes. Consequently, our inspection was pro forma and the guards soon raised the crossing gate to let us pass. Everyone found Yugoslavia's ambience a welcome relief from backward, repressive Romania. Although the Yugoslav houses looked much like those in Romania, the store shelves displayed more food and other goods. Our modern hotel in Belgrade offered a great meal and also entertained a well-known fellow guest—Sophia Loren was staying there while shooting a movie.

After this family trip in 1987, I visited Romania a third and final time. In 1991, I had business in Debrecen, Hungary, and diverted briefly to visit Joska Richter outside Oradea. After we had dinner together at his house, Joska put me up for the night with his son who lived nearby. As I was leaving the following morning, Joska said, "I have something for you." He handed me a package wrapped in newspaper and bid me farewell. I opened the package to find two pewter candlesticks that had belonged to my mother. Following our summary eviction to Mikoujfalu in 1944, we had left the candlesticks in our Hadad home. There was no room for them in the two suitcases that the government allowed us to take.

Joska's family obviously had stolen the candlesticks. Presumably they also had taken our other belongings after we were deported to the Nazi camps. All these years, Joska had held on to them without telling me. The candlesticks themselves had little monetary value, but they were family heirlooms—the only ones remaining—and therefore were precious. My father and mother used them on Friday nights and religious holidays to begin religious services before dinner. Upon returning home to New Preston, I placed one candlestick on the mantel in our dining room where we see it at every meal. I gave the other candlestick to my brother Gabriel, who presented it to his daughter, Debbie, on her wedding day. The return of the candlesticks was wonderful, but it begs the question: what did our neighbors do with the rest of our belongings? The very thought makes me sad.

Despite these three trips into Romania between 1981 and 1991, I still had no information about one other important Hadad family—the Banfis. In 2008, I inquired about them on the Internet and a respondent advised me to contact Arpad Meszaros, the priest in Hodod's Reformed Church. When I followed up, the priest informed me that Tomas, one of Count Banfi's two sons, lived in Cluj, and he gave me Tomas's telephone number.

When I reached Tomas by phone from my home in Connecticut, he immediately asked several questions without pausing for an answer: "What are you doing? Do you have enough money to live on? Do you know Joska Richter?" Apparently Joska, among others, had importuned Tomas for money, so he thought that I too was looking for a handout. After disabusing Tomas of his concern, I asked him how he was doing. Tomas reported that he had spent the last thirty years in a Russian gulag. He added, "I don't go anywhere. My mind and body have been destroyed." The Banfis had survived under the Nazis only to suffer under the Soviets. Although most of the Banfis' immensely valuable real estate has since been returned to them, they are in no position to restore and enjoy it.

I can never go back to Hungary or Romania again. Another visit would awaken too many painful memories. Furthermore, my family would not stand for it because of the long bouts of depression caused by each of my previous visits. I empathize with the undeserved suffering of Moses Adorjan, Uncle Mihaly, and Tomas Banfi under the Communists. But I resent the indifference of most Hungarians to the massacre of their Jewish population by the Nazis. They assisted the Nazis, or at least stood by passively, and then looted Jewish property. I grieve for the hundreds of thousands of Hungarian Jews who perished because of the cruelty of their fellow countrymen. I grieve for my lost family and friends, stripped of their lives and possessions by a malevolent Nazi regime and a compliant Transylvanian population and its government. With this memoir, I hope to convey both the grounds for these feelings and also the blessings of becoming an American citizen. How lucky I am to have survived the Nazi camps, to have escaped Romania, to have settled in the United States, and to have enjoyed the gift of a prosperous and happy life with a wonderful family.

EPILOGUE
Historical Perspectives and Personal Reflections

Using some of the enormous scholarship about World War II and the Nazi genocide of the Jews, I have tried to place my personal experience into the broader historical context. By April 1944, when the tragic aspects of my story began, Germany was on the defensive everywhere. Soviet Russia had broken the German siege of Stalingrad in February 1943, causing the surrender of the entire German Sixth Army, and also had won the massive tank battle at Kursk in July 1943. Kursk ended any prospect of German victory in the east. After liberating Leningrad (St. Petersburg) from a nine-hundred-day siege on January 27, 1944, Stalin called for a general Soviet army offensive against Germany from the Baltic to the Black Sea. The Russian offensive brought to bear its twofold advantage over the opposing German Army in military personnel and armaments. By May 1944, the Russians had liberated most of the Ukraine and Crimea and stood on the Romanian frontier at the foothills of the Carpathian Mountains, threatening a breakthrough into Hungary.

On its southern front, the German army was also fighting in retreat. In May 1943, the Afrika Korps surrendered, leaving North Africa to the British and American forces. Maintaining their successful offensive in the southern Mediterranean, the Allies invaded Sicily in July 1943, took the island by August, and landed at Salerno on the Italian mainland in September 1943. Later that same month, the Allies accepted Italy's unconditional surrender. In January 1944, the Allies made an amphibious landing at Anzio, which threatened to encircle the German Army holding the mountains further south near Monte Cassino. In March 1944, the Allies launched attacks at Monte Cassino and by April had advanced above Naples and established a front extending across the Italian peninsula.

On June 4, 1944, the Allies entered Rome, and on June 6, 1944, D-day, the Allies invaded France at Normandy. In anticipation of the Allied invasion across the English Channel into France, Hitler had begun withdrawing vital military forces from its collapsing eastern defenses in the spring of 1944. Despite its deteriorating military position, however, the Third Reich maintained, even accelerated, its Final Solution, which now included extermination of Hungarian Jews.

Following the Russian defeat of the Second Hungarian Army near Voronezh in January 1943, and the Italian desertion of the Axis cause in September 1943, the Nazi leadership became anxious about Hungary's continued loyalty. In the early hours of March 19, 1944, Wehrmacht forces entered Hungary along with the SS and Gestapo to begin the German occupation of Hungary in collaboration with the compliant Hungarian government and sympathetic Hungarian fascists. Two days later, Adolf Eichmann, commander of an SS Special Commando unit of 150 to 200 men, arrived in Hungary to implement the Final Solution. By decree of March 31, to be effective on April 5, 1944, the puppet Hungarian government adopted an SS directive that required every Jew above six years of age to wear a canary-yellow, six-pointed star on the left chest of his or her outer garment. Thus began a series of calculated steps to mark, isolate, round up, rob, and deport Hungarian Jews.

On April 4, 1944, in collaboration with Eichmann and the leadership of both the German Wehrmacht and Hungarian Army, the Hungarian minister of the interior completed the plan for rounding up Jews and collecting them in temporary ghettos throughout Hungary for eventual deportation to Auschwitz. The ministry first directed local mayoral and police authorities to require registration of all Jews, using local Jewish institutions to assist in the process. The plan then directed local police officials, assisted by Nyilas (members of the ultra-conservative, pro-Nazi Arrow Cross Party), to collect Jews from small towns and cities into local ghettos for transfer to designated holding areas. These holding areas were factories, brickyards, and other such places located near larger cities from which the Germans would entrain and deport the ghettoized Jews to Auschwitz.

In northeastern Hungary, the roundup began on the first day of Passover, Sunday, April 16. By May 10, the entire roundup was finished, with Jews throughout Hungary gathered into holding areas, referred to malevolently as the "mint." Police and Nyilas used these local ghettos to torture Jews into disclosing the location of their hidden valuables. In Hungarian Transylvania, the ghettoization drive began on May 3, and by May 10, 1944, included 98,000 Jews. Their deportation to Auschwitz commenced on May 15, with four trains running daily, each carrying 3,000 Jews. After force-marching the eighty to one hundred Jews of Hadad to the Szilagy Cseh train station, the local police and Nyilas shipped them north to a holding area in Szatmar. Between May 19 and June 1, the Germans transported the Hadad Jews by cattle car from Szatmar to Auschwitz.

Giving greater priority to the Final Solution than to the approaching Russian army, the Wehrmacht and German railways cooperated fully in this mass deportation by providing the necessary rolling stock. By June 8, 1944, the number of deported Hungarian Jews reached almost 300,000, and by July 8, the number totaled about 440,000—all shipped off to Auschwitz. Of that latter number, 350,000 were gassed immediately upon arrival at Auschwitz. Under pressure from Heinrich Himmler and Albert Speer, however, Hitler agreed to exploit 100,000 Hungarian Jews as slave laborers in underground bunkers and defense industries. Of this latter group of 100,000, which was spared immediate death and enslaved for the German war effort, only about 35,000 survived. Gabriel and I were among these relatively few lucky survivors.

The willingness of educated Hungarian Jews like my parents to accept their forced ghettoization and deportation is as understandable as it is disturbing. Since 1867, Hungarian Jews had enjoyed legal equality and good relations with the Magyar aristocracy. This Jewish "Golden Era" ended with World War I, when Hungary lost territory and Magyar population in Transylvania. Nevertheless, Jews generally considered themselves to be well-integrated Hungarian citizens, and also considered the emergent pro-Nazi, anti-Semitic Nyilas Right to be a temporary political aberration. This Jewish conviction persisted even after Hungary adopted a pro-Axis policy following the 1938 German Anschluss with Austria, and after Germany had delivered northern Transylvania back to Hungary in the Second Vienna Award of August 30, 1940. Hungarian Jews like my father believed that their long service to the Magyar elite, including their World War I service, would protect them. These Hungarian Jews were the so-called "Magyars of the Israelite faith." Indeed, until March 19, 1944, when the Wehrmacht entered the country, Hungary had protected its 825,000 Jews and even harbored some Jewish refugees from Poland.

Tragically, throughout the war, the Jewish leadership in Hungary failed to share with the Jewish community its growing knowledge of Hitler's Final Solution, and the Hungarian Jewish community failed to heed the Nazis' ominous anti-Semitic rhetoric. In mid-1941, officers of Hungary's National

Central Alien Control Office rounded up almost 16,000 "alien" Polish and Russian Jews in northeast Hungary and turned them over to the SS. The SS promptly robbed these Jews and ultimately massacred them by machine gun, disposing of their bodies in a mass grave. In January 1942, Hungarian officers, mostly of Swabian-German background and stationed in occupied Yugoslavian territory, force-marched over three thousand victims, including hundreds of Jewish men, women, and children, before executing them on the Danube strand. Although the Hungarian government brought these officers to trial in December 1943 following a public outcry, the defendant-officers escaped to Germany in January 1944, only to return two months later with the German occupation forces.

The Reform and Orthodox Jewish leadership had historically aligned itself with the Magyars and maintained its loyalty to the Hungarian nation, despite the mounting evidence of Nazi atrocities and adverse intentions toward Hungarian Jewry. As early as 1942, Jewish soldiers in the Hungarian Army on the Ukrainian front had witnessed and reported on the atrocities committed against Jews by the *Einsatzgruppen* (SS "action squads" formed for liquidation of Jews and other so-called undesirables). In early 1943, moreover, members of the Bratislava Jewish Council reported the existence of Auschwitz and other annihilation camps to the Hungarian Jewish Council.

In early 1944, several weeks before the German occupation of Hungary, the Bratislava Jewish Council further reported to the Hungarian Jewish Council the specific SS intentions for Hungarian Jewry. Furthermore, in April 1944, escapees from Auschwitz provided the Hungarian Jewish Council directly with detailed information about the tattooing, gassing, and cremating of Jews at Auschwitz over the prior two years. Notwithstanding their advance knowledge about Germany's death camps and imminent plans for annihilation of Hungarian Jews, the Hungarian Jewish leaders decided not to inform the Jewish community on the incredible grounds that it would incite a Jewish panic. Consequently, many local Jewish leaders, including educated Jews like my parents, never knew about the ongoing Nazi atrocities already committed against European Jews or the ghastly Nazi intentions for Hungarian Jews.

As early as 1940, while planning his invasion of Russia, Hitler had decided to solve the "Jewish problem" by killing all European Jews. Charged with developing an extermination plan, Reinhardt Heydrich submitted his Final Solution project in January 1941. On September 3, 1941, the Germans first experimented with the use of Zyklon B (hydrogen cyanide) in a small gas chamber at Auschwitz by killing about 850 people, mostly Soviet prisoners. In March 1942, Auschwitz-Birkenau began its systematic gassing of Jews. Because it was central to European Jewry, the Germans chose Poland as the site for its death camps and designated Auschwitz for exterminating the Jews of southeastern Europe. In anticipation of receiving hundreds of thousands of Hungarian Jews by mid-1944, Rudolph Hoess, the Auschwitz commander, constructed a new railway branch line and quadrupled his manpower in order to effectively implement his plan to kill 6,000 to 12,000 Jews per day.

The Germans decided to situate Berga Camp about sixty miles southwest of Buchenwald and fifteen miles south of Zeitz at a former textile factory near the Elster River. Whereas Buchenwald had a capacity of about 84,500 prisoners, Berga had a capacity of only about a thousand. In the summer of 1944, Lieutenant Willy Hack arrived with his SS administrative staff to construct the camp for slave laborers and to supervise the excavation of an underground tunnel complex intended as a secret production facility. On November 12, 1944, the first shipment of European Jews arrived at Berga. Archival records show that Gabriel and I (numbers 752 and 753, respectively) arrived at Berga from Buchenwald on December 13, 1944. (See photograph of manifest.) During Berga's short operation between November 28, 1944, and April 7, 1945, 313 prisoners died there. Furthermore, residents of the city of Berga could not have failed to observe the carnage, since the dead were carted in wheelbarrows through town toward what is now referred to as the Jewish cemetery.

On February 13, 1945, the Berga camp received 350 American prisoners of war captured during the Battle of the Bulge. I saw some of these GIs while working in the Berga kitchen. The Germans had segregated them from other American POWs for use as slave laborers—mostly because they were Jews or looked Jewish. Over their following six weeks at the camp, some Americans escaped, but about two dozen died and another two dozen became hospitalized. On April 5, 1945, these remaining American POWs, including the sick, embarked southward on a forced march guarded by twenty-eight elderly Germans from the National and Civilian Guard, under the command of Captain Ludwig Merz and Sergeant Irwin Metz. During the next fifteen-day march, almost fifty American soldiers died. On April 23, advance American forces accompanied by a Sherman tank finally liberated the 169 surviving Americans at the city of Roetz, near the Czechoslovakian border. After the war, Captain Merz and Sergeant Metz were tried for war crimes and served three and fifteen years' imprisonment, respectively. In April 1947, Lieutenant Willy Hack, the Berga commandant, was arrested by the East German government in Saxony. A Zwichau criminal court tried and retried Hack for war crimes and ultimately sentenced him to death. On July 26, 1952, Hack was executed in Dresden by hanging.

From the beginning of 1945 until VE Day on May 8, about 120 such prisoner marches took place throughout Germany in a last-minute Nazi effort to remove evidence of the camps while still continuing to exterminate the Jews. The first phase of the death march program, from January through March 1945, consisted of mass migrations from the Polish camps into Germany. The second phase, from March through the war's end on May 8, consisted largely of directionless marches toward death. The Germans who conducted the marches included SS camp guards, but many were ordinary civil defense or police units. Most of the guards who supervised our march from Berga fell into this latter category. Typically lacking any centralized control or clear destination, these guards relentlessly drove the emaciated, weak, and sick prisoners literally to death. Moreover, this senseless herding and killing occurred despite Himmler's instruction that the camp guards stop executing their Jewish prisoners and begin releasing them into the countryside. Himmler did not want to compromise his ongoing negotiations with the Americans. During these first four months of 1945, between 250,000 and 375,000 of the 750,000 remaining camp internees died on these marches.

The Berga death march began on April 12, 1945, and proceeded in cold snowy conditions over the Erzgebirge (Ore Mountains), which climb three-quarters of a mile above Berga-Elster. On April 21, 1945, the march reached Kovarska in Sudetenland, where the guards packed everyone into a barn during the snowstorm. The next day the guards divided the marchers into three groups, one heading toward Theresienstadt, another toward Plauen,

160

and ours toward Manetin, Czechoslovakia. Our group arrived in Manetin about April 23, left Manetin on April 28, and headed back into Sudetenland and turned south toward Pilsen, covering 130 miles total before being liberated on May 5 by Czech partisans. The German guards herded the helpless Jewish prisoners into and then out of Czechoslovakia, seesawing back and forth between the Russians approaching from the east and Americans from the west. Throughout the Berga death march, like the other death marches throughout Germany, guards continued to execute weakened prisoners who fell by the wayside or were unable to keep up the steady pace. Their relentless pursuit of the Nazi genocidal policy persisted despite Germany's retreating army and imminent defeat.

Considering that my personal story of the Holocaust took place over the very last year of the war, as the Allied victory over the Germans became ever more likely, the murder of my family and other Hungarian Jews seems all the more unnecessary and tragic. The malevolence of the Reich leadership, naïveté of the Jewish leadership, and passivity of religious and political leaders worldwide all contributed to this gruesome outcome. Throughout March 1944, Eichmann's Special Commando unit, in typical Nazi fashion, assured the Jewish community that they would not violate human or property rights while restricting the Hungarian Jewish population. On March 31, 1944, Eichmann expressly and falsely assured the Central Jewish Council that this mass incarceration of Jews was only a wartime measure: "After the war, the Jews would be free to do whatever they wanted." Furthermore, on April 19, 1944, even as the ghettoization and deportation continued, the German and Hungarian authorities granted the council specific, if hollow, legal authority over all Hungarian Jews.

Deprived of their traditional Magyar support under the newly installed puppet regime in Hungary, the Jewish leadership apparently felt helpless to do other than go along with these anti-Jewish measures. They simply hoped to outlast the Nazis. Had they done otherwise, no doubt the Nazi and Hungarian authorities would have replaced them. But perhaps the publicity surrounding their resistance to the Nazis would have alerted the larger Jewish community to its impending doom. Instead, like most Jewish leaders elsewhere in Europe, the Hungarian Jewish Council went along with their Nazi persecutors and kept their flock in ignorance. To this very day, their silence is deafening.

The Christian leaders in Hungary and elsewhere remained similarly compliant. Labeling most Jews as largely National Socialists or Bolsheviks and focusing their pastoral concern primarily on converted Jews, Christian churches, with some notable exceptions, generally supported the Hungarian government. Prominent among the exceptions was Bishop Aron Marton of the Transylvanian Diocese, who alone among the ecclesiastical authorities in that area condemned the anti-Jewish measures. Although long and fully apprised of the Nazi's Final Solution, Pope Pius XII declined to speak out against the German atrocities until June 25, 1944. Even then his message was weak and muted. He merely urged Admiral Nicholas Horthy, the Hungarian head of state, to try to ameliorate the "sufferings that have, for so long, been endured on account of their national or racial origin by a great number of unfortunate people."

The Allies' support for the plight of the European Jews consisted of belated and ineffective condemnation of the Nazi atrocities and unwavering rejection of any direct military intervention against the machinery of extermination. In a shameful reflection of their attitude toward the Jews, the United States and Great Britain declined to alter their restrictive immigration policies in order to aid the Jews. Furthermore, despite the urgent appeals of Jewish leaders worldwide to interdict the ongoing genocide, the Allies steadfastly refused, ostensibly for strategic reasons, to bomb the crematoria and railways leading to the death camps. Instead, the Allies planned to save the Jews by winning the war. In the meantime, however, their vocal policy efforts through the War Refugee Board, which began in early 1944, proved no match for the Nazi juggernaut.

By contrast, the heroic efforts by rare individuals like Hungarian Army Colonel Imre Reviczky and Swedish diplomat Raoul Wallenberg shine forth. As commander of a Hungarian Labor Battalion in 1944, Colonel Reviczky inducted, fed, and clothed any Jewish man, however young or sick, who entered his military headquarters. After the war, the Jewish community recognized his humanitarian efforts by citing him as "Righteous Among the Nations." On July 9, 1944, unfortunately only after Admiral Horthy had halted the Jewish deportations from Budapest, Wallenberg arrived there to provide forged Swedish passports for thousands of the remaining Hungarian Jews. For his humanitarian efforts on behalf of the Jews, the Russians in all likelihood killed Wallenberg at the war's end.

Reflecting on this entire experience, even after all these years, I fear for humanity. How could the civilized German people become so committed to an immoral Nazi authority and its evil policies that they would participate in genocide with no sense of personal guilt? The Wehrmacht jeopardized Germany's very survival by committing vital rolling stock and military personnel to the Final Solution rather than to its faltering war effort. They aided in the execution of Jews rather than recruiting Jews to support Germany's military machine. Ordinary German soldiers and police marched their helpless Jewish prisoners into Czechoslovakia directly toward the oncoming Russian army, deliberately placing their own lives in jeopardy in order to kill Jews. Carrying out Hitler's extermination policy seemed more important than saving their nation or even their own lives.

All of the religious and civil institutions that should have responded to the Nazi genocide consistently failed the victims. The Jewish Council, the Christian churches, the Papacy, and the American and British governments all found excuses not to act. What hope is there for our civilization if we cannot rely upon the great faiths and the great democracies to champion human freedom against the forces of enslavement and to protect the innocent against the will of evildoers? At this point in societal development, we should not have to rely solely upon the courage of a few to protect the many against the worst of mankind.

Had my family any idea of the SS intentions for the Hungarian Jews in April 1944, we could have taken steps to protect ourselves. Across the Romanian border in Arad and Bucharest, we had close relatives who could have sheltered us. In Mikoujfalu, where Father was temporarily assigned to serve as doctor, we remained unguarded and lived within walking distance of the Romanian border and the nearby Romanian city of Brasov. Some Jews obviously learned what was happening and bought their way out of danger. Therefore, vital information was in fact conveyed, but only selectively disseminated. By electing not to disclose its knowledge of the genocide to local leaders of the Jewish community, the Hungarian Jewish Council left the majority of Transylvanian Jews uninformed of their mortal peril. By the time we learned what lay in store for us, we were powerless to react and protect ourselves.

When all else fails, we should be able to look to our community, our neighbors, and our friends for support against the forces of evil. And yet it seems that when civic authority curtails or jeopardizes our freedom, those closest to us are often prone to support their government, or stand aside silently, or even take advantage of our plight for their own betterment. The Christian people of Hadad never challenged the deportation of their Jewish neighbors. Instead, they willingly acceded to it. They stood by when their respected doctor, who had cared for them faithfully and saved many of their lives, was deported with his family. Moreover, they plundered our possessions after our deportation. Even today, they carry on as if the annihilation of their Jewish neighbors was a matter of indifference. Hadad's synagogue was demolished after the war and its Jewish cemetery remains shrouded in weeds. Recently the Hungarian government made a disgraceful offer to pay each Holocaust survivor the sum of $75 for the loss of a brother or sister and slightly over $100 for each parent.

The United States spearheaded the so-called German and Swiss Settlements for the slave labor and looted assets of survivors living in the United States. But this too was sham retribution. State Judge Sidney Gribetz, appointed to manage distribution of assets, told me that survivors would receive "peanuts" out of the funds allocated to US survivors after payment of fees to the attorneys and involved organizations. Federal Judge Edward R. Korman awarded $4 million to attorney Burt Neuborne, who had agreed initially to work on the matter pro bono, while his clients, the Nazi victims, received almost nothing. Such current treatment by our former liberators leaves a continuing bitter taste.

In conclusion, I must reflect on my own survival—a miraculous confluence of many factors. Father's medical practice ultimately did not preserve him or Mother, but it may have saved Gabriel and me. By delaying our deportation from Hadad and enabling our transfer to Mikoujfalu, Father's medical credential placed us on a train to Auschwitz with many other Hungarian doctors. On our arrival in Auschwitz, Dr. Mengele initially segregated the doctors, as well as Gabriel and me, for a work detail rather than immediate asphyxiation and cremation. Fortunately, throughout our internment in Auschwitz, Buchenwald, and Zeitz, Father remained with Gabriel and me to provide us moral support, which lasted until December 1944, when the SS decided during the selection process at Buchenwald to ship him back to Auschwitz and murder him. Throughout our internment in the camps, Gabriel and I luckily had one another for support. Fortuitously, the SS officer at Berga selected me for KP duty. That duty not only relieved me from hard labor but also enabled me to smuggle extra food rations to Gabriel. Finally, my active childhood participation in Hadad's farm life strengthened my constitution sufficiently to survive septicemia as a child, slave labor as a camp prisoner, a forced march into Czechoslovakia, and pneumonia as an escapee.

My camp experience and the death of my parents and relatives as a young teenager have haunted me for the last seventy years. Throughout these years I lived mostly in denial, trying to suppress my anger and pain by total immersion in my active business life, with its chronic pressure and globetrotting. But my torment—while bedridden for several weeks in 1984, while visiting Romania three times between 1981 and 1991, and while wrestling with this memoir over the past decade—persists to this very day. As a result of the Nazis' criminal treatment of my family and me, I no doubt have suffered and still am suffering from post-traumatic stress disorder, a condition that my family has lovingly endured and that I hope this memoir will alleviate. Most of all, however, I hope that by adding my experience to the stories of other survivors, the sheer weight of the accumulated literature will move the civilized world to spare others from such trauma by remaining eternally vigilant against man's latent potential for evil. I remain convinced that we must give injustice no quarter, for its harm, once inflicted, can never be undone.

REFERENCES

Atkinson, Rick. *The Day of Battle: The War in Sicily and Italy, 1943-1944.* New York: Henry Holt and Company, 2007. (A recent comprehensive history and my source for information on the Italian campaign as of April 1944.)

Barta, Gabor, et al. *History of Transylvania.* Translated by Adrienne Chambers-Makkai, et al. Budapest: Akademiai Kiado, 1994. (A detailed and authoritative history and my source for ethnic conflict and population information on Transylvania.)

Braham, Randolph L. *The Politics of Genocide: The Holocaust in Hungary.* Detroit: Wayne State University Press, 2000. (A comprehensive and invaluable analysis of the Holocaust in Hungary, and my source on the subject.)

Case, Holly. *Between States*: *The Transylvanian Question and the European Idea during World War II.* Stanford: Stanford University Press, 2009. (A thoughtful exposition of twentieth-century Transylvanian politics.)

Clark, Alan. *Barbarossa: The Russian-German Conflict, 1941-45.* New York: William Morrow, 1965. (A detailed history of the conflict on the eastern front.)

Cohen, Roger. *Soldiers and Slaves: American POWs Trapped by the Nazis Final Gamble.* New York: Alfred A. Knopf, 2005. (My source for information on the American POWs at Berga Camp.)

Goldhagen, Daniel Jonah. *Hitler's Willing Executioners: Ordinary Germans and the Holocaust.* New York: Alfred A. Knopf, 1996. (A groundbreaking analysis of the role of ordinary Germans in Hitler's Final Solution and my source of information on the death camps and death marches.)

Overy, Richard. *Russia's War: A History of the Soviet War Effort: 1941-1945.* New York: Penguin Books, 1997. (A brief, authoritative history and my principal source for information on the eastern front as of April 1944.)

Sanborn, Anne Fay, and Geza Wass de Czege, eds. *Transylvania and the Hungarian-Rumanian Problem, A Symposium*. Astor: Danubian Press, 1979. (A pro-Hungarian discussion of Transylvanian history and politics, with some useful historical information.)

Schmidt, Christine. "Berga-Elster ['Schwalbe V']." In *The United States Holocaust Memorial Museum Encyclopedia of Camps and Ghettos 1933-1945*, vol. 1, *Early Camps, Youth Camps, and Concentration Camps and Subcamps under the SS-Business Administration Main Office (WVHA)*. Edited by Geoffrey P. Megargee. Bloomington: Indiana University Press in association with the United States Holocaust Memorial Museum, 2009. (An authoritative account of the Berga-Elster Camp and death march.)